COMMUNITY CELL GROUP

YOU'RE INVITED

This book is published by Ulrike Hunt

and available via www.lulu.com

ISBN 978-1-291-37646-3

CONTENTS: Living a better Story

Introduction

One evening after a cell leaders' meeting, a few months after our vicar of 23 years retired, some of us were chatting about church in general and about cell groups in particular. We felt that cell groups were working reasonably well, but recognised that some were working better than others. Some cells were facing challenges and some cell leaders were beginning to get tired and weary. We also noted that there was a significant percentage of people who were not in cells and wondered how best to encourage people to come to cells.

We had just had our first round of interviews for a new vicar and not appointed anyone. Our concern was that as we faced an extended time of vacancy, we did not want to cell groups just coast along, tread water or simply survive until a new vicar was appointed (and dealt with the issues cell groups were facing?) We wondered whether perhaps this time of vacancy, given that it was going to be longer than first expected, was the ideal opportunity to do something different – something that would boost cell groups, that would build community, that would provide central teaching which, unlike on Sunday mornings, people would also engage with in groups, something that would help us as a church get a grip on who we are before a new vicar arrived.

And so the idea of Community Cell was conceived.

Over the months to come we worked on this idea, hammering out a course content, handing in a proposal to the church leadership and praying about it. More and more, we felt that this was going to be a key season in the life of our church. More and more, we felt that God wanted to do deep things in us through it.

Many emails, coffees and meetings later we were ready to launch. Over 8 weeks before Easter 2013 we met in cell groups and yet together as a church, as a community.

On the whole, the course went really well. Actually, it exceeded our expectations! It exceeded people's expectations too judging by the feedback we had. People enjoyed coming to the evenings and got a lot out of it. Those who were somewhat reluctant at first enjoyed the course despite themselves! And those who were not able to come, were able to access the talks online.

Because the course was such a blessing to us who ran it and to those who came, we wanted to pin it down somehow. This book is the result!

PART ONE

The Talks
COMMUNITY CELL GROUP
WORD
YOU'RE INVITED

Setting the scene

We often think of God as being part of our story.

That is of course quite right. For many of us, God *is* part of our story.

But there is a sense in which we are part of God's story. Our individual and collective lives are part of a bigger picture! God is living his own story and we have an intrinsic part in that. God intended us to be part of his story, he has a purpose for us within the context of his story and he invites us to take an active part in his story.

Getting a grip on what God's story is then, is vital if we are to understand what *our* part in it is. Understanding what God's story is, is vital if we are to step into the fullness of what God's purpose and intention for us is.

Catching a glimpse of the bigger picture we are part of will change our perception of God, but also of ourselves. Seeing ourselves as part of God's story will help us to get a better grip on who we are, what God wants from us, and what we wants us to do.

That is why we have called this series *"Living a better story"*.

The aim of the course is to open our eyes to God's story and to see our part within that and to help us step more proactively into the fullness of all God has for us within his story.

Meet the
COMMUNITY CELL GROUP
Author
Who is God
and
what is God like?
YOU'RE INVITED

Meet the Author:

Who is God and what is God like?

In order to be able to unravel God's Story, we need to be clear about the God we are talking about.

The Bible speaks to us first and foremost of a God who is Love. It declares so! The Bible is full of stories in which God's Love is demonstrated and seen. It is also full of statements God himself makes which give us a glimpse into his heart. And it is full of the testimony of those who have experienced God' Love. John for example, one of Jesus' closest friends, states: "God is Love".

It is important to grasp that God *is* Love through and through. It isn't just that God is capable of love - he *is* Love. Love is the essence, the DNA if you like, of who God is. This means that he is unable to act in any other way other than out of Love. All he says and all he does is only ever motivated by and saturated with Love because he cannot be untrue to who he is.

Whilst we sometimes struggle to reconcile this concept with our experiences and our understanding of God, this is the bottom line. This is the fundamental truth upon which we unpack God's story. The truth that God *is* Love emerges strong and clear as God's story unfolds.

Before we go on, we need to be clear about what we mean by Love. The concept of Love has been badly damaged and distorted in today's world. The kind of love our world understands is only an inkling, a shadow, of the Love that *God* is. In our world, our understanding

of love is coupled with how we feel about someone or something, and how that person or thing makes us feel in return. In our world, love is often conditional - transactional even – often only given if the recipient of our love gives us something in return.

The Bible however underlines that Love, the Love that defines God, is unconditional – it simply gives of itself. This kind of Love is strong and unyielding, as strong as death itself and as unyielding as the grave. It is as tenacious, staunch and alive as a blazing fire which no amount of water can quench. (Song of Songs 8:6-7) The Love that defines who God *is* is patient and kind. It does not envy, it does not boast, it is not proud. Nor is it rude or self-seeking. It is not easily angered and it keeps no record of wrongs. The kind of Love that defines God does not delight in evil but delights in the truth. This kind of Love always protects. It always trusts. It always hopes and it never gives up. This kind of Love never fails. (1 Corinthians 13:4-7)

Within the framework of Love, God is also powerful and mighty. The Bible is full of God's attributes – his power, his gloriousness, his might, his mercy, his forgiveness, his provision, his compassion, his delight ... the list is endless! The Psalmists give a great impression of all who God is. He is omnipotent. He can do everything he chooses to do. He is omniscient. He is all-knowing and wise – he knows everything he chooses to know! And he is omnipresent – he is everywhere he chooses to be.

Elohim

The first indication we get about God comes right at the beginning in Genesis 1:1. "In the beginning, God ...". The Hebrew word for God here is *Elohim.* It is important to understand what this word describes because *Elohim* is a plural noun! The concept of the plural, more than one, is further underlined when the writer of Genesis reports God as saying: "Let *us* make ...".

Now the Bible makes it abundantly clear that there is only one God. God is at pains to impress this point on his people. "Hear, O Israel, the Lord our God, the Lord is *one*!" (Deuteronomy 6:4) This is a declaration God's people repeated often.

So how can God be one and yet plural?

The answer is found in the character of God, in his DNA, in who he *is* - Love. Love can only ever be expressed within the context of relationship. Love cannot exist in a vacuum. Love can only really exist when it is given and when it is received. Love requires that it is demonstrated. And so Love can only exist where there is relationship, where there is communion, where there is fellowship.

It follows that if God is Love, he *has* to exist within the context of relationship. God, *Elohim*, is a God who exists in communion. Then, as now, *Elohim* expresses himself as Father, Son and Spirit and as Father, Son and Spirit, *Elohim* lives in perfect communion and oneness with himself. These three expressions of God are expressions of one thing – Love. Father, Son and Spirit share the

exact same essence, the exact same DNA – Love. "The Son is the radiance of God's glory and the exact representation of his being," the writer of the book of Hebrews explains. (Hebrews 1:3) *Elohim* is One although expressed in three manifestations.

There are earthly analogies which, imperfectly, can help to describe this concept of three in one. Christians in Ireland used the analogy of the shamrock – one leaf consisting of three different leaves. Celtic Christians used a triangular symbol consisting of three ovals intertwined. Another analogy is the substance H_2O. H_2O finds expression as water, steam and ice. Three different manifestations of the same substance. Another analogy is that of a human being. Human beings are made up of body, mind soul, and spirit. This side of death, these aspects of a human being are inseparable and yet we can talk about them as separate aspects. One, united, inextricably enmeshed, and yet separately distinct.

So when the Bible introduces God as *Elohim* right at the beginning, the Bible reveals that God lives in communion and in fellowship. The kind of God who exists in communion demonstrates that Love is at the heart of who he is. In fact, it is only because *Elohim* is a community that He is able to *be* Love.

Love creates

The story of God and humanity begins when God chooses to create.

It is not surprising that *Elohim* should choose to create. One of the ways Love expresses itself is through creativity. To create is a natural expression of Love. And so because *Elohim* is Love, he created.

He didn't create because he felt the need to create those who would love him in return. Love is, after all, not self-seeking. He already lived in perfect and meaningful relationship.

Neither did God create because he felt the need for affirmation or praise. Love does not envy. Nor does it boast.

God did not create because he wanted to feel superior to something. Love is not proud.

Love is kind. Love delights to give. God created in order to be able to share his Love, in order to lavish himself. God created so that the created would be able to taste, enjoy and receive his wonderful, delicious, life-giving Love.

It is probably worth pausing at this point and allowing this thought to take root in our hearts. God delights in lavishing himself, in giving abundantly of who he is, in order that the recipients of Love should taste Love for themselves. He did not create humanity with the primary purpose that humanity should serve him or give him glory. He created humanity with the primary purpose that humanity should enjoy his Love.

The purpose of humanity

People sometimes wonder about what the purpose of life is. Why did God create us? Why are we here? What are we put on this planet to do? People who believe in a God wonder about what it is God wants from them. Many Christians believe that God wants us to work for him, that he wants us to serve him, that he wants us to worship him.

Whilst none of that is untrue, if God created out of Love, with the primary purpose of lavishing himself, his Love, on his beloved creation, those answers do not make complete sense. We have already seen that Love is not self-seeking, nor proud, nor boastful, nor conceited.

The Bible in its entirety indicates that God created humanity because he wants to include her into his Love and into who he is. He created humanity "in his image", with the ability to receive love and to give love. The Bible indicates that God's desire, God's dream, is for humanity to mature in such a way that she is so entirely defined by His Love that she too can become included into *Elohim*. God's purpose for creating humanity is to unite himself to her!

For many people this is a somewhat shocking thought. Is it not blasphemous to think that God would want to draw us into himself and unite us to himself? We do want to be clear at this point – we are not saying that we become God! We are only saying that it is God's desire to draw us into him, into his circle of Love, into the community of the trinity, into *Elohim*, to instil his essence into our hearts and to invite us into communion and partnership with him.

One of the leaders of the early church, Paul, talks about being transformed into the image of God. "And we all, who with unveiled faces contemplate the Lord's glory, are being transformed into his image with ever-increasing glory, which comes from the Lord, who is the Spirit." (2 Corinthians 3:18).

The Bible underlines the concept of God's desire to unite himself to humanity again and again. In John 17, Jesus talks at length about unity with the Father and with himself. In Genesis, God created man and woman and put them together, making them a unit that is not designed to be separated. Revelation ends with the picture of a wedding. It talks about God, coming to dwell with humanity, joining himself to her.

Early on in human history, God binds himself to his people with an unbreakable agreement, a covenant, a vow if you like. God speaks about himself in terms of a husband to his people, a lover, as one who yearns for his beloved, who longs for a deep and genuine love relationship with her. Marriage is at its heart an illustration of what God purposes with humanity. Paul grapples with this in Ephesians 6. As guarantee of this union with God, believers receive the Holy Spirit into their hearts, "who is a deposit, guaranteeing our inheritance" (Ephesians 1:14), like an engagement ring that symbolises the promise of marriage.

It is an astounding concept really – that God should want to unite himself to us and us to himself. That he

should long for us to be like him, for us to become transformed to a point where we can be one with him, full of his Love, defined and saturated by His Love, just the way he is. And yet this is what the Bible indicates.

Why does God do it? Why does he create with such a crazy purpose in mind? Ephesians 1:14 gives us a clue – it is "to the praise of his glory". Somehow his intention to unite us to himself glorifies him, shows up his grandeur, reveals his character and elevates him above anything else we know. His desire to create those who can mature into what he is like, into his essence, speaks volumes about the kind of God he is. What a glorious, incredible, amazing God!

It is our experience that when this truth takes hold in our hearts that our lives take on a new dimension, a new meaning, a new purpose which energises, strengthens, encourages and gives life.

Soaking in His Love

Here is the crunch. There is a difference in knowing God in our intellect and knowing God experientially. Knowing about God is not the same as knowing God.

We are invited to know God deeply, intimately, and to be immersed and drenched in him! We are invited to immerse ourselves in his Love, in his being! The word "baptise" means exactly that – to immerse, to drench, to soak, to pickle!

There is no formula of how we do that. We believe it begins with a desire for more of God in our lives, a desire for God to completely fill us with his Love. Some of us like to sit quietly and use our imaginations to visualise sitting in God's presence, allowing him to pour his love on us. Others of us prefer to do something creative which helps us to soak up his love. Others still like to listen to music as they allow their hearts to become immersed in his Love. Yet others of us prefer to meditate on Scripture which talks about his Love and allow the Scripture to penetrate deep into our souls. It will be different for everyone.

But the invitation is there to soak in his love and to let his Love completely envelope us and sink deep into our hearts. There is no striving, no working hard. There is just rest as we receive His Love.

And God's Love completely transforms. It purifies us, it cleanses us, it energises us. It is his presence in us, which takes hold in our hearts as we open our hearts to His Love, which distinguishes us from other people. His presence, His Love, rests on us if we allow it to, and it is that which marks us out and which sets us apart.

DISCUSSION QUESTIONS

There are a lot of questions below. You may want to focus on one particular one, rather than attempt to answer them all!

God

1. God is Love. Do you agree?
2. What do you make of the idea that God exists in community?
3. Why do we sometimes question that God is Love?
4. Can you trace the thread of God's Love throughout the Bible? Can you trace the thread of God's Love in your own life?
5. When was the last time you spent quality time in God's presence? When was the last time you spent time simply soaking up his presence, rather than talking at him? How easy / difficult is it to spend time in God's presence without an agenda? What would you most want to talk to God about if you were to spend time in his presence?

God's story

1. How do you respond to the idea that God's ultimate purpose is to include us into himself? What do you make of the idea that serving God or worshipping God is not his primary reason for creating us?
2. How might God be revealing himself to you through this session? Is there anything you feel he wants to say to you?

When the script flips

COMMUNITY CELL GROUP

What went wrong and why does bad stuff happen?

YOU'RE INVITED

When the Script flips:

What went wrong and why does bad stuff happen?

If it is true that God is Love, why is there so much evil in the world? Why does God not intervene in all the evil that is in the world? If it is true that God wants partnership with humanity, if it is true that he wants to include her into the community of the trinity, why does God sometimes feel so distant? Why does it feel so hard sometimes to work out what we are supposed to do?

And within those questions, already, there is the recognition that something has gone wrong with creation. The way things are now are not the way they are supposed to be or were created to be.

Now all of us I expect would point to Genesis 3 to explain what went wrong. Genesis 3 tells the story of how Adam and Eve ate of the fruit God had forbidden them to eat from, and that as a result sin came into the world.

Let's have another look at that episode in history and think about how that impacts our own stories.

The knowledge of evil

The first thing we have to note here is that the tree God forbade humanity to eat from is the Tree of the Knowledge of Good and Evil. It is worth thinking about the properties of this tree for a minute. The fruit of this

tree, according to what it says on the tin, gives knowledge of good and also of evil. And actually, the serpent affirms that. "You will be like God, knowing good and evil." God too confirms it: "Man has now become like us, knowing good and evil."

The problem is - the knowledge of evil is poisonous. The knowledge of evil poisons the human heart with death.

Einstein once argued that cold can only be defined in relation to heat i.e. cold is the absence of heat. Similarly, light can only be defined in relation to darkness – darkness is the absence of light. It is because there is light that we know what darkness is. He then went on to argue that it is the same with evil. Evil can only be defined in relation to good. Because there is good, we know what evil is. Evil is the absence of good. Actually, evil is the absence of God. Where God isn't, there is evil. And the knowledge of evil is poisonous.

Knowledge here is more than knowing something in your head. Knowledge here is understanding and experiencing. There is a difference between knowing lots of facts about a person and knowing that person. There is a difference between knowing about evil as a concept, and experiencing and tasting, evil. There is a difference between knowing in your head what the absence of God feels like and experiencing, tasting and understanding the absence of God.

And the absence of God is poisonous. Fatally so. Experiencing the absence of God kills.

And God knew that. So he warned humanity: "Don't eat of that fruit, otherwise you will die. Perhaps it won't

affect your body there and then. But your heart will be poisoned by it. And the result will be death, not only in your spirit, and your emotions, and your mind, but eventually in your body."

And of course God was right about the fruit! Adam and Eve ate of the fruit of the knowledge of good and evil "and their eyes were opened." Suddenly they realised and experienced what the absence of God was like. The knowledge of evil poisoned their hearts with death. And the knowledge of evil, by definition, broke humanity's relationship with God.

We often think that God's relationship with humanity was broken because humanity disobeyed God's instructions. That is of course true because at the heart of disobedience is an attitude of rebellion against God.

But there was more to the break in relationship between God and humanity than disobedience. God is bigger than our disobedience! The issue is that death and life do not mix. They repel each other, like opposite poles of magnets. The experience of God's life cannot mix with the experience of death. Goodness cannot mix with evil. The experience of God's presence cannot mix with the experience of God's absence. It is simply not possible.

And because a God of Love allows humanity the choice of whether to be in relationship with Him or not (otherwise he would not be Love!), God has to allow the consequence of choices made. In other words, if we choose to invite the experience of the absence of God into our hearts, the presence of God has to take a step back. The presence of God has to make way for the choice we make of allowing the absence of God in. Allowing the poison of the knowledge of evil – death - into our hearts means that there is less space for God's life.

And so experiencing evil, tasting of where God is not, inevitably breaks the relationship between God and humanity, not because God turns away from humanity in disgust at her disobedience, but because God cannot be where he isn't! God cannot be present and absent in the human heart at the same time!

The root of sin

Many of us have grown up with the notion that it is our wrong actions which breaks relationship with God. When we do things that go against God's rules, then God turns away from us because he can't tolerate disobedience. Many of us have grown up understanding that sin is the sum of all the bad things we do that go against God's rules and it is this disobedience to God's rules which drives a wedge between us and God. When we steal, that is sin. When we lie, that is sin. When we misuse sex, that is sin. When we kill people, that is sin. Breaking God's rules is sin and it cuts us off from God because God wants us to obey him.

And that is quite right. But I sometimes wonder whether we need to rethink our definition of sin in a way that is more in line with God's character!

It is not broken rules that breaks our connection with God, it is a broken relationship! Sin is a condition of the heart. Sin is the poison of the knowledge of the evil in our hearts. Genesis 3 points to the truth sin goes a lot deeper than a list of the things we do wrong.

It is important we get this the right way round. A sinful heart is a heart that is poisoned by the knowledge of evil, the experience of the absence of God. Our behaviour becomes sinful as a consequence of having a sinful heart. We do bad things, things that go against God's rules, *because* our hearts are sinful, *because* our hearts are poisoned.[1]

What breaks our relationship with God is not the bad things we do *per se*. What breaks our relationship with God is that we choose his absence.

Jesus confirms the view that sin is not broken rules but a poisoned heart. Jesus talked a lot about the human heart. "Where your heart is, there your treasure will be," he said (Mt 6:21). "Out of the heart the mouth speaks." (Mt12:34) "Out of the heart come evil thoughts, murder,

---

[1] In fairness, a lot of the rhetoric we use in churches in our liturgy and in our songs don't help. We tend to focus on our wrong behaviour. When we do confession at church, we are asked to recall the things we said, did and thought that did not match up against God's standards and we are encouraged to confess those and ask for forgiveness for those. And yet Jesus says to us, loud and clear – it isn't about your behaviour. Your behaviour shows up the condition of your heart. But it is your heart that matters. Of course it is good to confess our wrong behaviour. But confession is equally about agreeing with God, confessing, (the root of the word is to 'say with' someone) that yes, our hearts are poisoned with the absence of God which is why we did, said and thought the wrong things we did, said and thought.

adultery, sexual immorality, theft, false testimony, slander." (Mt 15:19)

Jesus points out that the seat of sin, the seat of wrong behaviour, is rooted deep in the human heart. "Guard your heart, for it is the wellspring of life" the writer of Proverbs says.(Prov 3:23) If the heart is not well, if the heart is poisoned by the knowledge of evil, if the heart is disconnected from the presence of God, then out of the heart will come the corresponding behaviour. Conversely, a heart that is saturated by Love and by life will produce behaviour that reflects this.

Now in Jesus' time the religious leaders were very hot on people living according to God's laws. Rightly so in a way because their point was that as God's people we need to live correctly.

Jesus however challenged them about this on many occasions. Outward behaviour doesn't concern God as much as the condition of the heart. The outward behaviour is symptomatic of the condition of our hearts and it is the condition of our hearts that is the problem. Before God, your heart is already tainted even if it has not translated into a specific behaviour yet. "You know it says in the law you are not to commit adultery. Yes? Well, let me tell you, if you look lustfully at a woman you have already committed adultery with her in your heart." "You know it says in the law, don't murder anyone. Yes? Well, if you harbour anger against a brother you have already murdered them in your heart". (Matthew 5) The condition of the heart is the determining factor here. It is the condition of the heart that God is concerned about.

Why? Because it is the condition of the heart that kills! Right from Eden, the sinful heart, the heart poisoned by the knowledge of evil, was God's concern. If you experience the absence of God, your hearts will be poisoned with evil and you will die. The poison of the experience of the absence of God will kill you. Being where God is not will kill you, being turned away from God will kill you. And the experience of the absence of God cannot coincide with the experience of the presence of God. You can't have it both ways! If we make space for that poison, the life of God has to go. God allows us our choices on this one because he will not force us into relationship with him.

Far-reaching consequences

Unfortunately, Adam and Eve's choice to eat from this fruit had far-reaching consequences. This wasn't only something between them and God, but something that affected every human being born from them. Genesis 5 tells us that children subsequently born to Adam and Eve were born in Adam's likeness. In other words, no longer is our heart in God's image, saturated and defined by Love. All of us born after Adam and Eve were born with this poison of the knowledge of evil lodged in our hearts.

And we know it. We all have the capacity to sin. We all have the capacity to lie, steal, slander, misuse sex, be greedy and so on.

Our choice in it all

Why didn't God stop Adam and Eve eating from the fruit? Why did he put it in the garden in the first place?

This brings us to the second thing we note from Genesis 3.

God didn't stop Eve because there had to be one place where Adam and Eve were able to demonstrate that their connection with God was their choice. It wasn't that God deliberately put temptation in their way to trick them or to test them. It was just that a God of Love chooses to give people the choice about whether they choose to love God back or not. The Tree of the Knowledge of Good and Evil was that place. Eating of that fruit effectively meant they chose to turn their backs on God. When as humans we turn away from God, God allows us that choice – and the consequence that goes with it, even if the consequences are fatal. God allows us genuine choice because he is Love. Love never bullies its way in, Love never dominates, Love never forces.

And of course a world in which all human hearts are poisoned with the knowledge of evil, in a world where God allows us choices, in which we can choose how we behave, there is a lot of injustice and hurt. Because our hearts are infected by evil, we steal, we lie, we are greedy for power, we dominate over others, we slander others, we trample others underfoot.

And so it is little wonder that we live in a world where there is such a lot of injustice. Where there is such a lot of sorrow, such a lot of suffering. We all live in the wake of our own choices, but sadly, also in the wake of the choices of others.

So when we ask what has gone wrong with the world, why there is such a lot of evil in the world, we do have to take a look at ourselves. Let's not blame God for the choices we make!

Judgment

If God is Love, does God not care at all? Does he just let evil people get away with it?

The Bible does talk about judgment and it is worth bearing that in mind. God will judge. But judgment is not about God imposing himself. Judgment is our choice. Judgement is the consequence that unfolds when we choose to turn away from God, when we choose to live not according to Love, but according to evil. Judgment is what unfolds as we allow sinfulness to take root in our hearts. Judgment is our response to God's warning.

God said: Don't eat from that fruit or you will die. Humanity ate of the fruit. Judgment came – in other words: "I have to let you have it your way. That includes the full consequences."

God describes the judgment on Adam and Eve. Women will have a hard time giving birth and raising children and being the partner to her husband she was

designed to be. Men will have a hard time making ends meet. These were not random punishments. These were the consequences of how the poison of the knowledge of evil would unfold for them and for humanity.

So again, when bad things happen in the world – let's not be quick to blame God. So much of what is going wrong in the world is the unfolding of the consequence of our collective turning away from God, the unfolding of our bad choices, the unfolding of allowing evil a place in our world.

The adversary

There is just one final point I want to pick up out of Genesis 3, a very crucial point.

A third character is involved in how the script flipped – the serpent. And we know that this serpent embodies Satan. The word Satan literally means "the one who opposes", "the adversary", "the opposition". We won't go into why Satan has put himself in opposition to God. There is not time here! But suffice it to realise and to understand that that is what he is. He is the opposer, he is the adversary, the enemy, the one who is in opposition to God.

And he is the enemy not only of God, but of all who live connected to God and under God's wing.

So he tempts Adam and Eve. "Go on! God is not really telling the truth! He is keeping things from you and short-changing you because he is afraid you are going to be like him. You can't really trust him. Trust me!"

And Adam and Eve listened to his temptation. This is really important in terms of the bigger picture.

Because humanity listened to the enemy and did what he said, humanity, in effect, dethroned God and enthroned the enemy. Instead of submitting to God, humanity submitted to the adversary, the enemy.

This had cosmic, drastic and tragic consequences. Now the enemy was in a position of authority and power. Because humanity listened to him and did what he said, it was as though he usurped the throne of earth. Jesus himself calls Satan "the Prince of this world". Satan has set himself up over this earth to rule and dominate over this earth.

The awful truth is that we are all caught up in a world where we are, in effect, hostages. It is as though humanity has legally (if unwittingly) elected Satan to rule over the world. The thing is, as dictator, he will not be deposed and none of us has the strength to depose him.

And again this explains why there is so much suffering in the world. Not only are we all capable of hurting one another and making life a misery for one another. We also live in a world where there is a dictator who is in direct opposition to God and who will do everything to prevent us from connecting with God again. We are trapped in a world where the enemy dominates over us and keeps us in our place as slaves through fear, through guilt, through lies. He is the Father of lies, Jesus explains.

The script has flipped – things have gone very wrong on this earth and it seems as though God's purpose for humanity is thwarted. As humanity we have tasted of the knowledge of evil. We know what is right but we also know what is wrong. Our connection with God is broken. We know what it is like where God is not. God can seem so very far away at times. As humanity we are trapped in the world in which the Evil One, the one who is opposed to God and opposed to any of us connecting with God, keeps us in our place through fear, and through lies.

No wonder things are so bad on earth! No wonder there is so much suffering, so much pain, so much grief, so much sadness. No wonder the world is full of injustice!

And God? Where is God in all this?

The enemy tries to tell us that we have blown it and that God has turned his back on us, that we have made our bed now we have to lie in it.

Nothing is further from the truth! "Nothing can separate us from the Love of God," Paul says in Romans 8.

The truth is that God could have chosen to turn his back on us. He allows us our choices after all. He could have wiped us all out – the flood in Noah's time showed he had the power to do so and who could blame him if that is what he chooses to do? He could equally have said: 'You made your choice, I will leave you to get on with it. Sort it out yourself. Get on with it.'

But he doesn't do either! He sees what is going on. His beloved has been duped and deceived. His beloved has been kidnapped and has been made a captive by the enemy. His beloved has been poisoned and is mortally ill. His beloved his completely powerless to do anything against the poison that has entered her heart, completely powerless against the kidnapper who has put himself in power over her.

And God is angry. As angry as you would be if your beloved, the object of your complete Love, has been taken away from you and is in mortal danger. In his heart there is wrath – rage against the way things have turned out.

Traditionally, many of us have grown up with the notion that God is angry with *us* for going against his ways. But the truth is - God is not angry with us. He is angry with the enemy and he is angry about how things have panned out.

Yes, ok, within the context of relationship, sometimes God disciplines us, just like as parents we discipline our children. And within the context of relationship, sometimes God does get angry with us, just like parents do sometimes get angry with their children.

But the wrath of God that we so often think is a result of our having upset God, is not directed at us. God is not an angry, vengeful God, ready to punish us because we have offended him, ready to make us feel bad for what we have done. No!

God's wrath is against the way things have turned out and against the enemy who has dared oppose him!

And because God is Love he does everything in his power to rescue his dearly beloved - even if it costs him his own life. God does not leave us to muddle through on our own. God does not turn his back on us. God's passionate Love for us is unchanged.

And so his rescue mission begins ...

DISCUSSION QUESTIONS

There are a lot of questions below. You may want to focus on one particular one, rather than attempt to answer them all!

Sin and sinfulness

1. How do you respond to the idea that sin is broken connection with God rather than broken rules?
2. How do you respond to the idea that it is the sinful condition of our hearts that causes our wrong behaviour rather than our wrong behaviour that makes our hearts sinful?
3. How do you respond to the idea that it is the absence of God's presence, the understanding of evil, which poisons our hearts?
4. To what extent do you recognise the poison of the knowledge of evil in your own heart?
5. How can we rid ourselves of the poison of sin in our hearts?

Living in a world of injustice

1. Where does injustice come from? Who's responsible for injustice?
2. What is God's response to injustice?
3. Can humanity bring about a world of justice?

Why does bad stuff happen in the world?

1. What is the root of the bad stuff that happens in the world?

2. What is God's perspective on the evil that goes on in the world? How does God's perspective shape our own perspective of the bad stuff that happens in the world?
3. What kind of characteristics can Christians have as we live in a world where evil happens? What is our role here?

The Ultimate Hero

What did Jesus come to do?

The Ultimate Hero:

What did Jesus come to do?

We broke off the story last week in an uncomfortable place: humanity has turned away from the God who loves her with a passion she hardly fully grasps. She has eaten of the fruit of the Tree of the Knowledge of Good and Evil and in so doing has been poisoned by it. Her heart is in a bad way. She has not the strength or the capacity to get rid of this poison that has lodged itself in her heart. Moreover, she has been captured, kidnapped, by the enemy, the one who is in opposition to God. He is holding her hostage, he has pulled her away from her Lover and he is lying to her about him, making her believe that He is no longer interested in her, that she has blown it, that He has abandoned her, lying to her about his character and preventing at all costs that she should turn back towards him.

But God, because he is Love, does not shrug his figurative shoulders and let her get on with it. He does not turn his back on her. His Love will not allow that. Neither will he destroy her. He is going to rescue her! God's story is essentially about a rescue mission. Right from the dawn of time God calls across to humanity – hang in there! I *will* come and rescue you!

And today we are looking at "The Ultimate Hero". We will look at just how God, because he is Love, bursts into human history and how he rescues his beloved humanity from the predicament she is in.

In order for us to understand the hero, we need to understand our human predicament. If we are to understand and embrace the fullness of God's Love, his grace and his mercy, we need to recognise the condition of our hearts – that it is poisoned by the knowledge of evil even before we have translated that evil into an action. It is by default turned away from God. We also need to recognise that we are captives, held hostage by a dictator who acts in opposition to God at every turn, and who will not let us go. We need to recognise and take stock of our own helplessness in the face of our sinfulness and in the face of the enemy who is holding us captive.

When we have understood our position, we can much better recognise the rescue plan God sets in motion right at the dawn of time – a long-term rescue plan.

First God creates a setting in which rescue can take place. To do that, he creates a people group – Israel - through which he will speak to the world and through which he will bless the world. Through Israel, God speaks to the world about connection with him and about what he is like. More importantly, through Israel, God speaks of and demonstrates rescue. Israel is like a token, a demonstration of the fullness and completeness of the rescue God has in mind.

This people group, Israel, demonstrates that it is possible to live in connection with God, even though there is an enemy. Through Israel, God reminds the world what life lived out of Love looks like. Through Israel, God

demonstrates that God is there and involved, that God has not turned his back on humanity, that God is Love.

On a practical level, Israel is the setting into which God's rescue comes.

If we are to understand fully what Jesus did and the full impact that his death and resurrection have, we have to bear Israel's story in mind. Israel's story is the backdrop of God's rescue mission. Think of the Passover for example. At Passover, Jewish people celebrate the exodus – the way God rescued his people from a powerful authority who has kept God's people in slavery. It speaks of a God who connects with his people and walks with them, whose glory accompanies them as they make their way to the Promised Land.

But this story is a shadow of a deeper reality, a deeper rescue.[2] The story of the exodus is a picture of how God will rescue the world from a powerful authority who is in opposition to God, who is keeping people in slavery. And of course Jesus himself chose the Passover celebrations to stage his own cosmic rescue act. The overtones here are clear!

Not only does Israel visibly demonstrate rescue, the Old Testament is moreover full of prophecies about this rescue act. Israel's prophets speak of someone who will come and who will rescue God's people – this person is

---

[2] Actually, much of Israel's story (not just the Passover) that we read about it the Old Testament, is a shadow, an example, an analogy of God's ultimate rescue of the world.

known as the *mashiach* (Messiah in English, *christos* in Greek, from where we get the word Christ.)

It is really important that we understand the Jewish concept of Messiah if we are to understand fully who Jesus was and what he did. We say it so quickly – Jesus is the Messiah. Jesus Christ (as though 'Christ' is some sort of surname!). But what does that actually mean? What is a messiah? What does the word Christ mean? What does it describe?

Messiah

In Jewish thinking the Messiah is someone who is anointed by God, sent by God, someone who would come from God himself.

There are some key aspects that define the Messiah figure: he would be someone chosen, anointed and equipped by God himself. He would be someone who would deliver God's people from their enemies. He would liberate God's people, free them from captivity and from oppression. He would be someone who defeats the enemy. He would be someone who would establish the kingdom and who would reign as king. His reign would be like it was in the golden age of King David. And he would bring peace.

There are probably more, but these are the most up front aspects of what the Messiah would do.

Unfortunately, as often happens, things can get misunderstood, usually when people start looking at the trees and not the wood. Over time, this promise of the messiah has also become misunderstood. The people of Israel began to think that the messiah was a political figure who would come and deliver the nation of Israel from oppression. At the time of Jesus, Israel had been under occupation for about 400 years, first by Babylon, later by the Greeks and then the Romans. People therefore thought the messiah would be someone who would get rid of the political oppressors and re-establish the kingdom Israel as it was during the golden age of King David. Many Jews still take this view today. They are still waiting for someone who will come and who will save the people of Israel from political threat and oppression.

But from God's perspective, the story is not about only Israel. It is about the whole world, the whole of humanity! It always has been and always will be! The whole of humanity needs rescuing, not from political oppressors, but from the Prince of this world. And the whole of humanity needs to receive the antidote to the poison of death. The whole of humanity is dying!

From God's perspective, the messiah is someone whom God would send, who is from God, who would defeat the Prince of this world, who would liberate God's people and pave the way into freedom which is only found in connection and relationship with God, who would establish God's kingdom and who would bring peace. *And* he would be someone who would take on himself the poison of death, who would take on our shame and our sin into himself, and give us the antidote to death – life itself. The messiah would rescue completely.

And this messiah, in the fullness of that word, is Jesus!

In a dramatic and supernatural act of sabotage, God breaks into human history and becomes, himself, a man. It is completely wonderful. Awesome! And the more I think of Jesus, the more I meditate on the fullness of what he came to do (which is a lot more and a lot deeper than my sins being forgiven!), the more I realise just how pivotal Jesus is. He really is the pivot on which the whole of the human story revolves, the pivot on which God's story and our story meet. Everything hangs on him. No wonder God will exalt him and give him the name which is above every name (Phil 2).

The question we have to ask ourselves at this point is: why was Jesus necessary? Was it really necessary for God to make himself human, to die a horrendous death of torture, in order to rescue the world? Was there no other way? Could God not have simply intervened? Could God not just have removed the satan and ousted him from the world? Could God not simply have healed humanity's sinful heart, simply removed the poison from her heart so that she was not infected by death? Could God not have simply forgiven without the bloodshed of an innocent man? Could he not? Is God not Love, after all?

Well, yes, God could have done all the above in the sense that he is powerful enough to have done so. But if he had done so, he would have been untrue to himself – and God cannot do that.

We have already seen that God is Love and that because of that he had to allow humanity the

consequence of her choices. If God had barged in and ousted the dictator, if he had barged in and made everyone take the antidote to the poison of death, he would not be acting out of Love because he would, in effect, be overriding humanity's choice. God ties himself to his character, to Love, and it would be an illegal operation for him to defeat the enemy and save humanity from death as God. Because God is Love, God, as God can't just change the matrix.

But God as man – that is a different matter!

Jesus' humanity is actually really key when it comes to God's rescue act. God becomes human because as a man he is a representative of the human race. As a man, he has every right to take on the enemy and depose him, as a man and as the representative of the human race he has every right to dethrone the dictator. And as a representative of the human race he has every right to take on death.

And so, in a supernatural act of sabotage, God becomes a man. Jesus is not just God dressed up as a human, disguised as a human. Jesus is not just God with skin on. No! Jesus is completely divine in the sense that his essence is God's. He *is* Love, his DNA is Love, just as God *is* Love. But he is also completely human. This is what we marvel at at Christmas when we think about a virgin conceiving a child - the Holy Spirit himself came on Mary and allowed her to conceive a child in the perfect image of God. A child who is completely human and yet is completely in the image of God. We cannot help but wonder and marvel at this mystery.

God becomes man in Jesus. Jesus is the perfect and most complete human being. He is completely full of God, full of His Love. And so there is not a trace of the poison of death in him.

Actually, Jesus embodies God's purpose for humanity! This has immense implications for us as his disciples because what it means is that Jesus models the 'normal Christian life' for us. We are invited to live just as Jesus did and do what he did because everything he did, he did out of his humanity, not out of his divinity!

He defeats death

Jesus then is the way God rescues humanity. He is the ultimate hero!

He takes on death. Death had no hook on him. Jesus says so himself: "No-one can take my life from my but I lay it down of my own accord." (John 10) And he willingly lays down his life. He allows himself to be killed. But because death had not poisoned him, because his heart was completely free from the poison of the knowledge of evil, death could not hold him. And gloriously, triumphantly he came to life again, completely defeating death!

What that means for us is that if we hide ourselves in Him, if we open our hearts to him, if we allow His life to flow into us, through the ministry of the Holy Spirit, then death has to step back. Just as life had to step back when we turned our backs on God, now death has to step back as we turn towards God and receive the fullness of His Love, as we receive his Life into our hearts. There is so much more we could say about this – how this life burns away the poison in our life and the fact that it is a process ...

The fact that Jesus defeated death also means that if we have his life in our hearts, then death has no hold on us either. Ok, our bodies might die, but that is meaningless really. Our hearts are alive and connected with God. 1 Corinthians 15 talks gloriously about how Jesus is only the first one to come to life again but we will follow him. We too, our bodies too, will come to life again. Death is defeated. The sting of death is gone! The poison in our hearts is burned away by the life Jesus breathes into us. Thank you Jesus!

He defeats the enemy

Jesus doesn't only take on death – he also takes on the enemy. Through his resurrection, he defeats the power of the enemy over us. He buys us back. The ransom the enemy wanted was our very lives. Jesus paid the ransom with his own.

Jesus triumphs over the rulers and the authorities in the unseen realm. (Colossians 1). The enemy insisted he had a claim on us – Jesus bought us back, redeemed us from the enemy's clutches. We are free! Because of Jesus' resurrection and his triumph over death the enemy has no right over us anymore. We are no longer hostage to his lies, to his deception. We are free!

Again there is so much more we could talk about – how the enemy lies to us and makes us think that he still has power over us...

He enables the Holy Spirit to come

Somehow Jesus' resurrection and ascension opened the way for the Holy Spirit to make his dwelling within each person who puts their trust in the fact that Jesus is the messiah who has saved the world. Jesus explained very clearly (John 14 - 15) that the other Helper, the Holy Spirit, would only be able to come once Jesus was glorified. In Old Testament times, the Holy Spirit would indwell particular people, who were chosen for a particular task, such as prophets. Or he would come on people on particular occasions. We read of the Spirit falling on Saul or on David, for example. Yet after Jesus' ascension, the Holy Spirit falls on and indwells all believers. Why? Because he represents Jesus to us. He ministers Jesus to us, reminding us of what Jesus taught and did. It is through him that we are equipped to be his kingdom's agents in this world.

He establishes the kingdom

And Jesus, because he overcame the enemy, is now the rightful king over the earth. He is the prince of peace, the king of kings and the Lord of Lords. And he will establish God's Kingdom in the physical realm as it is in the heavenly realm, on earth as it is in heaven.

The thing is – this bit of his messianic role has not yet been completed. The kingdom of God has not yet been fully established on earth as in heaven! Jesus has defeated the enemy but the enemy is still very much alive at this point in the story. But Jesus is the Messiah! The Bible assures us that Jesus is the victor and that there will come a day when he will come again in victory, as Prince of Peace, as King. Then he will completely destroy the enemy, and then the kingdom of this world will be superseded by the Kingdom of our God and of his messiah. (Revelation 11:8)

Then the enemy will be ultimately defeated and have no hold on anyone ever at all anymore. Then there will be no more injustice, no more death, no more tears, no more suffering.

But that is still to come. The story is not over yet. The ultimate hero has dealt the decisive blow to the enemy – to Satan as well as death. But the story is still going on and we are caught up in the middle of it.

We live in the middle of the clash of kingdoms – the Kingdom of God which Jesus heralds, proclaims and announces and the Kingdom of darkness over which Satan exercises his power. The Bible tells us that God's kingdom will emerge triumphant and that one day God's reign will be on earth the way it is in heaven. In the meantime, the kingdom of the prince of this world wars against it. Victory is assured, but there are many battles still to be fought!

We, as agents of His kingdom whose allegiance is to the Prince of Peace and the King of Kings, are living, as rebels, within the kingdom of the prince of this world.

The good news of Jesus

This promise of God's kingdom, of God's rule extending over earth the way it is in heaven, this is our good news! This is the gospel - Jesus is the messiah, he is the victor who will completely defeat the enemy's hold over this earth and he is the one who will establish God's Kingdom and God's reign. The way things are now on earth is not the end of the story! The good news is, there will be a time when everything in heaven and on earth will come under his rule!

When Jesus was alive, his overriding message was: "The Kingdom of God is near!" That is the good news he wants us to declare loud and clear today.

When we take stock of this whole thing – first of all our predicament as humanity and then how God, through Jesus, so gloriously rescues us – surely we cannot fail to bow our knees in worship and in thanks to Jesus. He really is the only one who can save. He is the messiah! He is our ultimate hero!

DISCUSSION QUESTIONS

There are a lot of questions below. Again, you may want to focus on one aspect, rather than cover all the questions.

Jesus as the ultimate hero

1. How is Jesus the only one who can save the world from the predicament it is in?
2. How does Jesus fulfil his role as the "Messiah"?
3. Are there ways in which Jesus is a hero that you had not considered before?
4. What is your response to Jesus?

The Power of the Cross

What exactly did Jesus achieve through his death and resurrection? How is Jesus' death and resurrection more than about our sins being forgiven?

The good news

Mark 1:15 "Jesus went into Galilee proclaiming the good news of God. 'The time has come,' he said. 'The kingdom of God is near. Repent and believe the good news!'"

1. What is the central message Jesus told his disciples to tell people? What does that mean?
2. How is the good news from God so much more than the offer of sins forgiven?

The Right Cast and Crew

The importance of community

The Right Cast and Crew:
The importance of Community

Why community?

In session 1 "*Meet the author*" we discussed that God exists in community. Even before he created the earth and humanity, he already existed in perfect, complete and loving community, the community that is *Elohim*. Community then is central to who God is and therefore to his story because community reflects who God is.

The trinity shows us what community is like. Father, Son and Spirit are always pointing to each other, glorifying each other. At Jesus' baptism the Father openly declares that Jesus is his beloved son with whom he is really pleased. After his baptism, Jesus submits to the direction of the Holy Spirit and follows him into the desert. During his earthly ministry Jesus often points to the Father and declares that he and the Father are one, united, of one mind. He also talks about God glorifying him. (John 8). He promises the Holy Spirit to his followers to make up for the fact that he, Jesus, will not be there any longer. And so it goes on. *Elohim,* the community of the trinity, give us the perfect example of what loving community looks like.

Invited into the community of the trinity

As we have said before, God's intention and purpose is to invite us to be a part of his community. God did not create humanity in order to satisfy a need he had, or

have those who would worship him or glorify him. He already had that! He already existed in perfect completeness. God did not create the earth and humanity out of self-centredness, because he was self-seeking or because he was egotistical. God is none of those things. Paul, writing to the Corinthians, tells us that Love is not self-seeking, nor boastful, nor proud. Nor did God create us because he was bored. God created humanity because he is Love, and Love seeks to give and share.

In Genesis 1 and 2 we read how God created humanity in his own image. Everything God created, the earth and everything in it, God created well. "And it was good," the Bible tells us. But only humanity received the label "very good"!

Perhaps this is because God created humanity (and only humanity!) in his image – with the ability to receive love and to give love, the way he too loves and is loved. Just as God created birds to fly, God created humanity to love and to be loved.

Jesus, the night he was betrayed, prayed an astounding prayer, which reflects the heart of God's intention of including us into his community. "My prayer is not for them alone," Jesus prays. "I pray also for those who will believe in me through their message, that all of them may be one, Father, just as you are in me and I am in you. May they also be in us so that the world may believe that you have sent me. I have given them the glory that you gave me, that they may be one as we are one – I in them and you in me – so that they may be brought to complete unity. Then the world will know that you sent me and have loved them even as you have loved me. (John 17:20 – 23)

It is an incredible prayer. And if it wasn't for Jesus saying so, if it wasn't for the Bible tracing God's purpose like a red thread throughout its books, one might be forgiven to think that such an idea is heretical and even blasphemous. And yet, God makes his intention very clear – you are invited to be part of God's community, to be one with Him just as Jesus is one with him.

The human community

Because community is so central to God, God puts community at the heart of humanity right at the beginning. After God created Adam, God said: "it is not good for man to live alone." Although God had labelled the human being as "very good" and although nothing had marred creation in any way, God stated that it was not good that man lived alone, with no human mate. Adam was living in perfect communion and relationship with God, and yet God gives Adam a human mate, one that he joins himself to and becomes one flesh with. It is quite clear – we are not meant to be alone. We are meant to be connected with one another, because that is what God himself is like.

Because community is at the heart of who God is and therefore at the heart of God's purpose and design for humanity, God wired humanity in such a way as to

function best when humanity lives in communion with each other.

The purpose of community

We would do well to think about the importance of community and to begin to grasp just how important community is for humanity. After all, Jesus said: "The world will know that you are my disciples if you love one another." (John 13:35) In a world marred by sinfulness, a loving community of people demonstrates more than anything else, what God is like.

God puts community at the heart of human existence, not only because it is a reflection of his own existence. God puts community at the heart of human existence because it is through community that God's heart is revealed. A loving human community is a direct expression to the world of how much God loves us and how God loves us. It is a visible demonstration to the world about his purpose and his intention for humanity.

Church programmes are all very well, but Jesus didn't die so we could do church programmes! In our churches we talk a lot about how to do discipleship and evangelism, we work out the best way to run our youth programmes and cell groups and that is all right and good. However, we often forget that the base line is community and that community the way God intended is completely unique in this world. We forget that it is essentially through community that we will show the world how much God loves people! Jesus died so that we could be part of God's community! And

because of that, community is at the heart of how God wants us to show the world how much He loves them.

Realistically...

Having said all that, it is abundantly clear to everyone that as humans we find community very very difficult. Building up a loving community as God intended is hard work and very costly to us.

Henri Nouwen comments that "community is the place where the person you least want to live with always lives".

Why? Not because it is a difficult thing for humans to do. No. God created us to thrive on community. We are wired to love and to be loved. We are wired to be interdependent.

We find community difficult because we live in a matrix in which our hearts have been poisoned by sinfulness and by death. We live in a matrix in which we all have a tendency to be independent and self-centred, in which we have a tendency to be out for self. This tendency is a symptom of a world which has experienced the absence of God's Love, which has turned away from God and is not connected to the God who is community.

We also find community hard because none of us are perfect. We upset each other and we allow ourselves to become upset by others. The truth is that we are all damaged and dented by the sinful matrix we live in.

On the 'reduced shelf' at the supermarket, there are lots of goods that are 'damaged goods'. There is something not quite right, not quite perfect about these goods – a multipack short of a packet of crisps, a dented tin of beans, a leaking tub of soup. And the truth is all of us are like the items on the 'reduced shelf' at the supermarket. All of us, without exception, though admittedly some more noticeably than others, have got something wrong with us, some area of life that we struggle with, something that eats into us and reduces our capacity to love and to be loved.

The trouble is that we have a tendency to assume other people are not damaged and we expect them to live and react perfectly. We don't allow others to be the damaged people that they are.

Building an 'as is' community

In America, the reduced shelf at the supermarket is called the "as is" shelf. You have to take the goods on that shelf as they are, as you find it.

If we are serious about community, if at the heart of things we want to live in loving community in our churches because that is what God calls us to do, then we would do well to consider one another as "as is" goods. We cannot afford to go around thinking that we are the only ones that need special care while everyone else should be more able to get on with things. Nor can we afford to go around thinking that we are normal and because of that everyone else should be too. We need to recognise that everyone is a little

weird, everyone is dented, everyone is damaged at some point of their lives.

The New Testament talks a lot about building community despite our damage. The early church spent a lot of ground breaking years trying to work out how, now that Jesus (the Messiah, the Christ) had triumphed over the enemy and over death and sin by his resurrection, community would look like. For the first time, the community of God's people was now no longer confined to the people of Israel. It encompassed Gentile believers too. Paul says: "Now there is neither Jew nor Greek, slave nor free, male nor female for you are all one in Christ Jesus." (Galatians 3:28)

And so we find many exhortations in the New Testament, that call us to "make every effort to keep the unity of the Spirit through the bond of peace" (Ephesians 4:3). Note how Paul exhorts us to make 'every effort'. This encompasses much more than a quick 'hello' on a Sunday morning.

"Bear with each other, and forgive whatever grievances you have against one another," Paul writes to the Colossians. (Col 3). "Be patient, bearing with one another in love." (Eph 4)

And that is our challenge as we build up a community that reflects God's Love to a broken world, as we build community out of a bunch of damaged and broken people – to work on it, to treat one another with grace, to look to each others' needs more than our own. It is our challenge to work on relationships, not to allow relationships to sour or fall apart.

And it is each of our responsibilities! It is not up to someone else, or the vicar, to sort things out and to build community. It is for each one of us, who is touched by God's Love, to do our bit in building community.

John Ortberg comments: "To allow or contribute to disunity is to be fundamentally at odds with the purpose of God in human history. It may be common in our world but it is not normal in God's eyes."

How do we get the capacity to build loving communities that reflect God's heart?

First and foremost, we must all be open to receive God's Love. Out of our own efforts, none of us have the capacity to love in the way that is required to demonstrate a loving community to the world.

But God does not expect us to do this in our own strength! He wants to fill us with His love, to saturate us with his Love. And as we receive and are filled with his satisfying and wonderful Love, we receive the power and the capacity to love others, even those who are damaged and dented and "a bit weird". Only when we have allowed God to saturate us with His love, do we have the capacity to build loving communities in which we love others the way Jesus loved us.

DISCUSSION QUESTIONS

There are a lot of questions below. You may want to focus on one particular one, rather than attempt to answer them all!

Invited into the community of the trinity

1. What do you think it means to be included into the community of the trinity? What might that look like?
2. What is our part in becoming included into the community of the trinity? How much depends on us?

The importance of community

1. How do you respond to the idea that a loving community reflects God's heart and God's nature?
2. In what way does a loving community reflect God? In what way is it the way God draws people to himself?
3. "Learning to live in loving community is more important than having programmes for evangelism". Do you agree? Why or why not?

Building "as is" communities

1. What are the obstacles to our building loving communities of damaged and broken people? What stops us doing so?
2. What needs to change within your group / your community / church in order for your community to become more and more a loving community? What do you personally need to do? What is your part in building this kind of community?

Learning our Part

What is the point of church?

Learning our part:
What is the point of church?

What is the church?

In order for us to fully understand what the purpose of church is and what her mandate is, we need to grasp the story so far. We need to think about church within the context of the bigger story in order to be able to get a hold on what the church is and what church is (supposed to be!) about.

The story so far ...

So let's just recap the story so far: God created us for and out of Love. His ultimate purpose for humanity is to draw her into the community of the trinity, into his very being. However, as a result of humanity turning away from God and experiencing evil, the human heart is poisoned by sinfulness and death. Moreover, Satan, the opposer, deceived humanity into giving him the authority over the world. Satan has enthroned himself over the world and keeps humanity hostage. But God doesn't turn his back on humanity. He is determined to rescue her - whatever the cost - from death and sinfulness and from the power of the enemy.

Jesus embodies God's rescue mission. Jesus heralds God's kingdom, stating that it is near (and that it is here!). He demonstrated and explained what life looks like within God's kingdom and under God's rule. Through his resurrection, Jesus defeated death, and

thereby also sinfulness (because death is the consequence of sinfulness). Through his resurrection he also overcame the enemy. Jesus is and will be the rightful king of this earth.

Whilst he has not yet established his kingdom fully on earth as it is in heaven, the Bible assures us that he *will* return to earth and destroy the enemy (and sin and death) completely and utterly. So today we find ourselves in that time where victory is assured, but the war is not yet over ...

What is the point of church?

Church, then, is intrinsically part of God's story. In this season where victory is assured, where Jesus has defeated death, and triumphed over the enemy and has the antidote for sinfulness, the church is God's way of demonstrating these truths!

Dietrich Bonhoeffer, a German 20th century theologian and martyr, describes the church in this way: "The Church of Jesus Christ is the place, in other words the space in the world, at which the reign of Jesus Christ over the whole world is evidenced and proclaimed."

In other words, within the context of God's story, the church is a community of people who are invited to herald and demonstrate God's reign, the way Jesus did when he was on earth.

Jesus is the rightful king of this earth. That is the truth of it. That is what he achieved on the cross. And one day he will return and establish God's kingdom on earth as it

is in heaven. Jesus himself taught his followers to pray this into being: "Your kingdom come, your will be done on earth, as it is in heaven." God's rule, God's dominion, God's reign will one day visibly extend over the whole of the earth.

The Bible tells us that the kingdom of this world (or the kingdom**s** of this world) will be superseded by the kingdom of God. (Revelation 11:7) The Bible tells us that every knee will bow and every tongue will confess (that means "agree"!) that Jesus, the messiah, is indeed the King of all kings and the Lord of all lords. (Philippians 2:10-11)

The church's role, then, is to herald this Kingdom, to herald God's reign. The good news the church has to share is that the way things are now in this world (injustice, suffering, grief, sickness, pain and so on) is not the end of the story. The good news the church has to share is that a time is coming when evil will be defeated for good. A time is coming when God will be king.

In what way should the church do that? Through preaching, through teaching and through demonstrating the truth of God's kingdom!

The church is in a unique position to *herald the truth* about God's kingdom and what things are like in God's kingdom. There are many examples in the Bible of the power of proclamation – the power there is in declaring the truth. The church has a powerful truth to declare (and New Testament writers come back to this again and again): "Jesus, the messiah, *is* Lord!" He is the one

with authority, not the enemy! He is the one who reigns and who will reign over the earth with justice and truth. Whilst the fullness of this is not yet, the church is in a wonderful position to be able to proclaim it loud and clear to the world, but also to the powers and authorities in the unseen realm. Jesus, the messiah, the Christ, is the King of kings and the Lord of lords!

Then the church is called to *demonstrate* what things are like in God's kingdom. In God's kingdom there is no sickness – so Jesus calls his church to minster healing and health and wholeness. In the Kingdom of God there is no grief – so Jesus calls his church to heal the broken hearted, to inspire hope, to minister wholeness and inner wellbeing. In the Kingdom of God people are valued and all are welcome – so Jesus calls his church to be a community of people that welcomes everyone.

We could write chapters and chapters about what this might look like (and there are plenty of books which have been written about this topic), but the underlying challenge is – how do we proclaim God's reign and demonstrate what things are like in God's kingdom in our locality? How do we demonstrate to a watching world that there is a different reality, as yet unseen, but nevertheless a reality, where God reigns?

Finally, the church is called to teach about all this. The church is to *explain* to people that the realm where God is king will, one day, because of Jesus, impact earth too. The church is to explain who Jesus is to people, to talk to people about what his message was and what he did, and to explain to people just how

Jesus paved the way for us to be part of God's kingdom. The church is to explain to people that through Jesus everyone is invited to become citizens of God's kingdom, and to explain to people how to become a citizen of God's Kingdom. The church is called to explain and to demonstrate to people what being a citizen of God's kingdom means and what that looks like. In short, the church is called to make other disciples.

Not long before he was taken from our sight, Jesus said: "All authority in heaven and earth has been given to me. Because of that, go and make disciples of all nations...". (Matthew 28:19-20). Not converts, but disciples – those whose allegiance is also to Jesus; those who will also follow him and do what he did and proclaimed what he proclaimed; those who in turn will tell others about who Jesus is, about God's kingdom, and about how to become part of that.

So what is the church?

The church then is not an organisation, nor a building, nor a system, nor a religious order.

The Bible tells us that the church is a living body, in fact it is a body that re-presents Jesus. The Bible goes as far as to say that the church is the body of Christ (Ephesians 5:23, Colossians 1:24). In other words, the church is a body that is supposed to be what Jesus was when he was on earth. The church is supposed to do the things he did!

The church is a living organism, not an organisation.

The church is a house built up of living stones, not a building. (1 Peter 2:4-5)

The church fulfils a role that priests fulfilled in the story of Israel. In Israel's history, priests were people who were set apart from the rest and who were distinctive. They were to act as intermediaries between God and the world. The Bible tells us that the church is a royal priesthood – a group of people who are different to others, who set the tone in worshipping God and pointing to Him, and who represent God to the world and the world to God. (1 Peter 2:9-10)

Lastly, in Revelation 19:7, the church is described as the bride of the Lamb (in other words, Jesus). "For the wedding of the Lamb has come, and his bride has made herself ready." (It is clear from the context of the whole of Revelation that the bride is those who have steadfastly clung on to Jesus and followed his ways.)

Various scholars and thinkers have described church in their own way:

- The church is *koinonia*, a living community of people who love each other, who share their lives on a deep level and who reflect God's purpose of community.
- "*Koinonia* rests entirely on the degree to which the faithful are intimately united to their Lord and to one another." (Tavard)
- It is a "gathered community of sinners called to be attentive to God." (Peterson)
- "A successful church is one that loves Christ." (Stackhouse)

- "The church has the ability to transform culture." (Niebuhr)

Fulfilling her mandate

As we have already seen, the church is a community of people who proclaim, teach and demonstrate the reality of God's story. We just want to pick out a couple of key points with regards to how the church is called to fulfil her mandate.

God's intention for his people on earth is to bless others. When God called Abram with the intention of creating a people group from his descendants, God said: "I will make you into a great nation, and I will bless you; I will make your name great, and you will be a blessing. I will bless those who bless you, and whoever curses you I will curse; and all peoples on earth will be blessed through you." (Genesis 12:1-3)

God doesn't bless Abram to reward his faithfulness or his trust in God. He blesses Abram *so that* he will be a channel of blessing to others.

We see this principle again and again throughout the Bible and it is a fundamental principle in God's Kingdom – when God blesses, he does so, not for our own sakes but for the sake of others. When God blesses, he expects us to channel that blessing to a hurting and confused world.

The church is called to live out that principle. The church is to be a blessing, not a curse, to a broken world – a community which reaches out to others,

which inspires hope, which demonstrates the reality of a different kingdom, God's kingdom, and helps a hurting world to glimpse that.

When Jesus started his public ministry on earth, he quoted the prophet Isaiah as his "manifesto": "The Spirit of the Sovereign LORD is on me, because the LORD has anointed me to proclaim good news to the poor. He has sent me to bind up the broken hearted, to proclaim freedom for the captives and release from darkness for the prisoners, to proclaim the year of the LORD's favour and the day of vengeance of our God[3], to comfort all who mourn, and provide for those who grieve in Zion - to bestow on them a crown of beauty instead of ashes, the oil of joy instead of mourning, and a garment of praise instead of a spirit of despair." (Isaiah 61:1-2)

As followers of Jesus, as those who do what he did and proclaim what he did, Jesus invites us to take up the same purpose: to proclaim good news to the poor (not just financially poor!), to bind up the broken hearted, to proclaim freedom (from sin, from the enemy's clutches) to those who are captive, and to shine the light of hope into those who are imprisoned (by their own choices, by what others have done to them, by what life has done to them) to proclaim that God loves us and that God

---

3 We often get confused about this and think that God will take vengeance on us! But God's vengeance is not directed at his beloved humanity! God's vengeance is directed at the enemy although there is a sense in which his vengeance does extends to those humans who have wilfully refused to be rescued, who persistently align themselves with the enemy. He will avenge his beloved who has been abused and made hostage!

will deal with the enemy and with sin and death, to comfort those who are in despair and who mourn (not just if they have lost a loved one!) and to look after those who grieve....

So the church is called to love others and to be a blessing to others. How does the church become a blessing to the world?

In order to be a blessing, the church must first receive blessing.

It is only when we allow the Holy Spirit to indwell us and to make his home in our hearts, that we receive the power to live as kingdom agents. It is only through the Holy Spirit in our lives that we have the capacity to demonstrate what things are like in God's kingdom – to extend healing and wholeness to people, as Jesus did. To teach boldly that Jesus is king. To live connected to a reality that is super-natural, that is above what we perceive with our natural eyes. It is only through the Holy Spirit's empowering that we receive power to be a blessing to others

Similarly it is only when we receive and experience God's Love, that we are able to love others in the way God loved us. It is only when we open our hearts to God's Love that we have the capacity to love recklessly and unconditionally.

When Jesus was on earth, he talked a great deal about loving against the odds, loving our enemies and those who bully us or persecute us, loving those who are unlovely or even unlovable.

And Jesus made a startling statement, the night he was arrested, just after he had washed his disciples' feet: "A new command I give you: Love one another. As I have loved you, so you must love one another. By this everyone will know that you are my disciples, if you love one another." (John 14:34-35)

The church then is called to reach out to others in love. By loving, against the odds, through service, through laying down our lives for others, the world will see that our allegiance is to Jesus, the one who saved the world and is King over all kings. "Live a life of love," Paul encourages the church. (Ephesians 5). Walk in the way of love, make love your goal!

As well as loving others, the church is to love God too. To love the one who loves her unconditionally, who has done everything in his power to rescue her from the poison of sin and death and from the enemy. To love the one who gives her life. To love the one whose purpose it is to draw her into himself and to unite himself to her. To love the one who sanctifies her – burns away the residue of poison in her heart, who transforms her into his bride.

Reality check ...

The question that we must ask ourselves at this point is: why does my church look nothing like this?

Many Christians struggle with church. Many of us don't particularly like going to church. We struggle with how things are done, we struggle with the structure of the

organisation, we struggle with the way it is led, we struggle with miscommunication and fractured relationships, we struggle with all sorts of things.

And many of our struggles have their root in the nagging sense that what we do is perhaps not what we are supposed to be doing and that how we do church is perhaps not the way church is supposed to be.

And it may be that over the last two thousand years we have lost sight of what church is supposed to be about, that we have lost sight of who exactly we are following and that we have lost sight of our mission. We have got caught up in the structure and outworking of church and forgotten how to express the heart of it within the context of our generation and in the context of the times we live in.

And perhaps we need to take the time and the space to re-think church. To re-think who we really are and what Jesus' mission for us is. To re-think in the light of that what we do and how we do it, to think again about why we do what we do in the light of the bigger picture, in the light of God's story.

The truth however is that God loves the church. He loves the community of people who have surrendered to him, who love him and who want more of him. He loves the community of people who have agreed to submit to him and have chosen to give him their allegiance. She is his bride and he will unite himself to her! Then as now, he invites her to be involved in heralding and demonstrating his kingdom. He invites her to partner with him in establishing his Kingdom!

DISCUSSION QUESTIONS

There are a lot of questions below. You may want to focus on one particular one, rather than attempt to answer them all!

What is the church?

1. Which image of the church the Bible gives us captures / excites you the most?
2. Why would God want to partner with you (individually / in your cell / in your church / in the global church)?

The mandate of the church

1. What distinguishes the church as being different to other communities in our town? In the world?
2. How can we as a Church get better at loving one another?
3. In what ways do we herald and demonstrate a different kingdom?
4. To what extent have you allowed the Holy Spirit to empower you to be an agent of God's Kingdom?
5. "The local church is the hope for the world". What do you think of that statement? How true is that in your town?
6. In what areas of your life might God be challenging you to herald a different King / Kingdom than the world offers?

Your part within the church

1. Is it possible to be a Christian and not meet with other Christians at church (i.e. in the building and during a service)?
2. Is it possible to be a Christian and not be part of the church?
3. 1 Corinthians 12: 7 – 31: every part of the body is important. What area within the Body of the Church do you feel you serve and apply your gifts to? Are you happy with this?
4. Ephesians 4: 11-13. Why should the Body of Christ be built up?
5. What examples does Paul give of how Christians should live their lives? (Ephesians 4:17 – 32) How important is this for mission?

Getting real about church

1. Where do you struggle to love the Church?
2. What can you do to resolve the struggles you have about church?
3. In what way is your church stepping into the purpose God has for church? What is your church doing really well?
4. In what aspects do you feel your church is missing the point with regards to God's purpose for church within his story?
5. What are some positive ways you can help shape the way your church operates?

Getting the Edit right

Life and the choices we make

Getting the edit right:

Life and the choices we make

Within the context of God's story, the bigger picture we are part of, the choices we make play a significant part.

We have already seen that because God is Love, he allows his beloved choices as well as their consequences. Giving humanity free will – the ability and the freedom to make choices – is a mark of God's Love. Love does not bully. Love does not insist on its own way. Love does not dominate or dictate. Love invites.

God allows us our choices because God is not interested in robots. God longs for genuine relationship with his beloved humanity. God longs to include us into the community of the trinity. That is an astounding purpose and intention for humanity and not one God imposes on those he loves. God gives us the choice of whether we want to become part of his circle of Love, or whether we choose not to be.

But if God gives us genuine choices, he also has to allow the consequence of those choices. If God overrode the consequences of our choices, God would not be acting out of Love. He would not really be allowing us our choices if he consistently overrode them, and their consequences.

The consequences of our choices and the outworking of those choices is essentially what judgment is. God allows us our choices, but also the genuine consequences of those choices. His judgment is the outworking of our response to his invitation.

The people of Israel for example, saw God's rescue in supernatural and miraculous ways. God's intention was to give them the Promised Land straight away after their rescue from Egypt from where they would be a blessing to others. But Israel decided not to trust God about that. When the spies came back from their rekkie trip, the people chose to listen to some of the scaremongering stories going round, rather than to God's promise that they would be able to take the land with very little resistance.[4]

However, Israel's stubborn refusal to trust God meant a 40 year stint in the desert. A journey which could have taken 11 days, where God had already prepared the land ahead of them, now took 40 years. As a consequence, there was much bloodshed and violence when Israel did finally get to the land God had purposed for them. Their choice affected not only a

---

[4] God had told Abraham centuries before that "your descendants will come back here, for the sin of the Amorites has not yet reached its full measure". (Genesis 15:16) In other words, once the sin of the Amorites had reached its zenith, once their chance of turning to God had reached a point of no return, then judgement would come on them. In their case it would mean Israel's taking over of the land. The Bible intimates that the people groups living in that land knew that God was giving the land to Israel. The Bible seems to imply that the take-over of the promised land would be fairly straight-forward, with the people fleeing before Israel, rather than Israel having to battle their way through.

generation of Israelites, but also the people to whom they were supposed to become a blessing!

And so, within the context of God's story, our choices are significant. God gives us the choice about how we respond to the invitation he gives us. God gives us the choice as to how we act out our part within his story.

God invites us into partnership with him. As we wait for his mission to be completed, we are invited to be his partners in heralding and demonstrating his kingdom. But it is up to us whether we accept this invitation and challenge, or whether we ignore it. The level at which we follow God, obey him and submit to him, serve him and partner with him is completely our choice. God invites us deeper, but never bullies us into doing something against our will.

We can trace this principle all through the Bible. Abraham was invited into partnership with God when God saw his level of faith and decided that Abraham was the perfect candidate through which to build a community of people who could witness to the rest of the world about relationship with God. The Bible tells us that Abraham chose to believe God, Abraham chose to trust God (mostly!), and God credited his faith to him.

Jonah was invited to partner with God in opening the eyes of the people of Nineveh to God and to call them to turn back to him. Jonah refused – he knew God would have mercy on the Ninevites and Jonah didn't want God to have mercy on them. So Jonah chose to run away. God kept inviting him back into partnership, because God is gracious and eventually Jonah did

choose to agree to it. But even there he had a choice. He went to the Ninevites, but he went grudgingly and resentfully. That attitude too, was a choice (which God has a chat to Jonah about).

Even Jesus had a choice whether to submit to God's purpose or not. In Gethsemane we find Jesus wrestling, to the point of sweating blood because of the choice he had before him. He would gladly not have gone through with the cross. But he chose to trust God and to submit to His will rather than insisting on his own. When Peter cuts off the High Priest's servant's ear, Jesus tells Peter off and states that he could, even now, call down twelve legions of angels who would rescue him from the arrest and the impending execution. But he chose not to call time out.

Choosing to submit to God's will, choosing to love God, choosing to hunger for God and to get to know him better, making good life choices – that is a kingdom value.

It's all in your mind!

It is really important to understand the power of the mind and of the will when it comes to making good choices.

Proverbs 23:7 talks about the power of the mind: "For as a man thinks, so he is." Romans 12:1-2 talks about renewing our minds. Jesus spent a lot of time discussing the importance of the heart and choosing to pursue treasures in heaven rather than worldly wealth.

Paul, writing to the Philippians, urges us to align our attitude according to Jesus'. "Your attitude should be the same as Christ Jesus." (Phil 2:1) The Greek word describing our attitude (*phroneo*) includes everything we think, feel and do.

The truth is that everything we do first begins with a thought. Choice happens in the mind. Claiming that "someone made me do ...." is not a valid claim – most of the time we have a choice in the matter! The same goes for the way we feel. It is no good saying: "I can't help how I feel." The truth is – you can! Or at least you can help what you do as a response to how you feel. You can let things govern you or you can choose to govern your own actions and thoughts. The truth is that we have the choice with regards to our thoughts, feelings and attitudes. It is a matter of the will and of the heart.

We are not victims! Jesus died so that we are free from the enemy's lies and his terrifying hold over our lives. Jesus died to give us freedom and to free us from the way guilt, or self-deprecation, or lack of confidence, or other people's opinions hold us captive.

Barriers to making good choices

Making good choices, especially when it comes to attitude, is not easy and is a daily challenge. There can be barriers to our making good choices and to our being able to fully use our free will.

Sinful behaviour is one of these barriers. There are times when we wilfully and deliberately repeat sinful behaviour, or a particular sinful pattern. It is quite possible to be in a habit of particular sinful behaviour to the point that we no longer remember that what we are doing is sinful. However, the consequence of sin is death. When we sin we empower the enemy and something dies. And so persistent sinful behaviour can become a barrier to our making good choices. God allows the outworking of that sinful behaviour and we live in the wake of those consequences. And living in the wake of sinful behaviour makes it all the more difficult to make good choices.

Having a rebellious will is another barrier to making good choices. There is a difference between being strong willed and being rebellious. Being rebellious is all about allowing your will to be set against God. It is choosing not to trust in God, choosing to disagree with God, choosing to disbelieve God. Rebellion has its root in pride. We see this in the story of the Tower of Babel, where the people decided to build a tower that demonstrated the way they had set themselves up against God. The Tower of Babel is a visible sign of the people's rebellion against God: we don't need God, we can rule the world ourselves, we can even unite ourselves and prove to God that we are just as powerful as he is.

Rebellion also has its root in fear. We are afraid of what will happen if we allow God to take control of our lives. So we baulk and rebel and chose the stance that says: "I don't trust you. I am setting myself up to stand up against you." Or we take things into our own hands and do things differently to how God has told us to do them.

Another barrier to making good choices is having had our will dominated or crushed, for example through abuse, or through having been bullied, or through having been manipulated, talked down to or consistently disrespected. Having had our will bruised, and even crushed like this, can breed cynicism. It can result in a critical spirit, one that is not open to persuasion but is stubborn, bitter and resentful.

Breaking the cycle

The good news of course is that we are not doomed to remain trapped in our bad choices or in a destructive pattern when it comes to making choices.

One of the most powerful things we can do to break the cycle is to repent. This is not a reeling off of our past failures. Repentance isn't about saying sorry for the wrong things we have done. Repentance involves a change of mind. It is a genuine recognition that we need to make a U-turn in our lives and walk in the other direction. Nor is this a one-off event but a continual reflection, a continual assessment. Repentance is a rhythm of a lifestyle in which we allow the Holy Spirit to convict and to break the power of the past.

To break the cycle of making bad choices you have to take active steps in the opposite direction. Forgiveness, for example, is a choice and an act of will. Forgiveness is not pretending that something didn't happen or that it didn't matter. Forgiveness looks at the damage and yet chooses not to hold a grudge against the perpetrator for it. Forgiveness is picking up the pieces but not allowing those pieces to destroy you. And to do that requires an act of will, a choice, to walk away from wanting revenge or vindication.

Repentance is also all about agreeing with God about where we find ourselves. Disagreeing with God about the truth of things in our lives can be a real barrier to repentance and breeds that rebellious spirit.

And of course God has plenty to say about us, not in a negative sense, but positively. Knowing what God says about us, knowing and believing the truths God speaks over us is incredibly powerful. The truth sets you free, Jesus once said. The truth that you are loved. The truth that God has loved you with an everlasting and unconditional love. The truth that God delights in the way you turn to him and take hesitant steps to pursue him. The truth that God has redeemed us and has called us by name. The truth that God invites us to partner with him and work with him in what he is doing, that he has things for us to do. The list is endless!

With the Holy Spirit empowering us, (which in itself is a choice!), we have the strength to "take every thought captive" (2 Cor 10:5) – before we open our mouths! With the Holy Spirit empowering us we have the strength to replace the rubbish in our minds with good and wholesome things (Phil 4:8). By the empowering of the Holy Spirit we have the capacity to be "living sacrifices" (Romans 12:1-2) who don't keep crawling off the altar but choose to submit to God. And of course submitting to God is the way to resist the devil in a way that he has no other choice but to flee from us. (James 4:7)

Psalm 103 talks about choosing to praise God, and to run past our minds what he is like, choosing to remember the way he has demonstrated his goodness and love in the past. Remembering and testifying to what God has done in our lives is hugely powerful. Revelation 12:11 talks about how the power of the saints' testimony is instrumental in defeating the enemy!

Surrounding ourselves with people who testify to God's goodness and choose to trust God, who build up and encourage, rather than tear down and destroy is another powerful tool when it comes to breaking the habit of bad choices and making good choices.

There are times when a person may need deliverance and release from evil influences. It may be that other Christians need to pray for a person and, in the power of the Holy Spirit, break evil cycles and strongholds in a person's life. There is not really scope here to talk about that at length, but we did want to briefly mention the reality that at times extra prayer and counselling is necessary.

However the underlying truth remains that God will not override our choices (although he will redeem our bad choices if we ask him to!) He will not make choices for us or live our lives for us. We need to do our bit in turning to him and choosing to make good choices. But he promises to help when we call on him.

The underlying truth also remains that he invites us to choose to step into his story. He has a role for us within his story, as a church and as individuals and it is our choice whether we step into that or whether we don't. Stepping into the fullness of what God has for us, trusting God fully and following Jesus completely, turns our lives into an exciting adventure! But clinging onto life, clinging onto control of our lives, not daring to step out, stifles and creates boredom and frustration. Jesus himself says: "Anyone who loves their life will lose it, while anyone who hates their life in this world will keep it for eternal life." (John 12:25)

RESPONSE TIME

Identifying the choices you make

1. Think about the areas in which we make choices (attitudes, response habits, television / internet / reading habits, relationships, career, use of time ...) Think specifically about the choices you face within those areas, especially in areas you struggle with.
2. Make a note of the choice you are making today in regard to that situation. Ask God to help you with your resolve.

The choices we have made

1. Think about some of the poorer choices you have made in the past. Agree with God that they were poor choices. Ask God to take away the guilt associated with those choices and resolve to "sin no more". Ask God to mitigate in the consequences of those choices, ask him to make something beautiful out of the mess you made.

Barriers to making good choices

1. Think about the things that prevent you from making good choices. List them on a piece of paper.
2. Burn the paper (or throw it away) as a declaration that you will not allow these things to undermine how you choose!

Jesus made choices

1. Read Philippians 2:5-8, Hebrews 12: 1-4, Luke 2:51-52, Matthew 26:38-39. Think about the choices Jesus had. How did he choose each time? What was his overriding guideline in how he chose?
2. Ask God to help you take courage from the way Jesus chose.

Editing the Script

Called to greater things

Editing the Script:

Called to greater things

We have already underlined that God invites us to be part of his story. God's story is one of rescue – he will rescue the world and the humanity he loves with a passion from sin, from death and from the clutches of the enemy. He will establish his rule, the realm where he reigns - his kingdom - and unite humanity to himself, as he has always purposed right from the very beginning.

And God invites us to take an active part in his story. Not only does he invite us to be rescued. Not only is our part the part of the beloved who is rescued. God subsequently invites us to become agents of his kingdom, whilst still in enemy-controlled territory (even though that enemy-controlled territory is rightfully his!).

We have already underlined that church is all about a community of people who love God and who have allowed God to rescue them. The church is a community of people who live in the light of Jesus' victory over sin, over death and over the enemy. It is a community of people whose mission is to love others as Jesus loves them and to bless a broken world by heralding a different kingdom and by demonstrating that different reality of God's reign.

God invites us to be his Kingdom's agents! *We* are the church! We are those who re-present Jesus on earth, as though we are him! The church is like his body – his physical presence on earth. We are Christians – "little

Christs"! Someone once said: "While you have breath left in your body, God is not done with you yet!"

Taking stock of our gifts

So as we step out into our role as Kingdom agents, many of us consider what we can bring to this role. What are our gifts? What is our particular role as an agent of God's kingdom?

Some of us struggle with this - what can we possibly bring that is of any value? What exactly are our gifts? When we read the lists of gifts listed in the Bible, we struggle to find ourselves within them. And we ask ourselves – what exactly does God want me to do? Where is God leading me? What exactly is my job? Am I brave enough to do it? Do I have the ability to do it? We question ourselves, we question our abilities, we question what we can bring.

Research has shown that people's number one fear is not failure, or rejection, but to have lived a meaningless life. We transpose this fear onto our Christian lives – we want our lives to count for something. We do want to be involved in God's story - but how exactly?

This chapter is not about helping us determine what our gifts are. There are plenty of other books that have been written about this. This is also something close friends (or your cell group!) have a role in – they are the best placed to help you see what you are good at, what talents you have and how you might put them to use.

This chapter is about looking further. It seems to us that when we think along the lines outlined above, we are starting from the wrong starting point. We are perhaps asking the wrong questions. The above questions, though entirely valid, are introspective. They focus on you, and on what you can bring. We want to raise your perspective to look to Jesus and what he wants to do through you.

Ordinary people with extraordinary calling

The Bible makes it clear that God does not invite people to step into particular roles because of their abilities or their merit. God does not seem to be in the business of choosing people of influence! Instead, he chooses ordinary people, with ordinary lives, to become extraordinary agents of his kingdom.

He chose Abraham, not because Abraham was an amazing father of many sons, but because Abraham demonstrated incredibly deep trust in God. Abraham acted on what he trusted and believed, not on what he saw. And God can work with that.

God chose Moses to lead the people of Israel out of Egypt, not because Moses was an amazing leader. Moses struggled with speech! Moses said of himself that he was not good with words or good at speaking! (Did he have a stutter?) And yet God was able to do incredible things through Moses because Moses was a humble man. He submitted himself to God's purposes and said "yes" even though he did not see how he could possibly do what God was calling him to do. And

God can work with humble people who submit to his calling.

He chose Joshua to lead the people of Israel after Moses, not because of his amazing skill in war. Joshua was not even a warrior! God chose Joshua because Joshua was someone who had dwelt in God's presence. He had been Moses' assistant and rarely left the tent of meeting – the tent where God met with Moses. And God can work with people who seek his presence and his glory.

God chose David, not because of his amazing skill with a slingshot or because of his courage. He chose David because David, in the secret of his heart, cultivated a heart of worship and a heart that drew near to God. God called him a "man after his own heart!" God can work with people whose hearts are drawn to and hunger for his own.

The Bible is full of other examples. And these people were just going about their regular business, doing ordinary things, when God calls them to something greater, to a bigger purpose – a purpose that dovetails with His story.

These people were by no means perfect. Abraham lied (the same lie on at least two occasions!), Moses murdered a man and David committed adultery. But it seems that God is less concerned with the things we do, and much more concerned with our hearts. God can redeem and bend our mistakes to his purposes, however awful they are – as long as our hearts are aligned with God's and we have said "yes" to the calling God has on our lives.

It also seems that God is interested in the journey as much as the destination. In other words, God is not only interested in us once we have perfected ourselves. God is interested in walking with people, equipping them and working with them as their lives and his story intertwine. God loves the journey! He loves the process of partnering with ordinary human beings! He loves the process of working in us, of refining us and drawing us deeper into him.

This should give us a lot of courage. Rather than write ourselves off because we are too ordinary, or because we have made too many mistakes, or because we have no special abilities, we need to recognise God's invitation to ordinary people who have made mistakes and are just going about their daily business, with no particularly special abilities. The truth is that God calls *all* of us to something greater, to a purpose in line with his story. "For we are God's workmanship, created in Christ Jesus to do good works, which God prepared in advance for us to do." (Ephesians 2:10) He calls us to align ourselves to Him, to bind ourselves to Him and to trust him. And when we choose to do that, God can work with us, even (and particularly!) in our ordinariness.

Called to greater things

Jesus said a very startling thing before he died: "Truly I tell you, whoever believes in me will do the works I have

been doing and they will do even greater things than these, because I am going to the Father." (John 14:12)

Going to the Father meant that Jesus was in a position to send the Holy Spirit on to each of his followers, those who really do want to work with him and be his Kingdom's agents. The Holy Spirit equips Jesus' followers and empowers them supernaturally. It is through the Holy Spirit that Jesus' followers are able to do even greater things than Jesus has been doing!

When Jesus was on earth, he healed the sick. He raised the dead. He cleansed lepers. He drove out demons. He preached about God's kingdom and explained what things were like under God's rule. And now he has called us, his followers, his body on earth, to do the same – and more! We, you and I(!), are called to heal the sick, to raise the dead, to cleanse lepers, to drive out demons and to preach about God's Kingdom! As God's Kingdom's agents we are to be a blessing to others.

Before we panic about that, let's remember the bigger picture. We are called to live supernaturally, through the empowering of God's Holy Spirit in our lives. But the aim of doing these greater things is not the things in themselves. It is not about how many people you will manage to heal. It is not about what you can do! It is not about us! The aim of these greater things is to reveal Jesus. To reveal God's Kingdom and Jesus as the King!

Those who want glory for themselves through living supernaturally will miss it all (and end up losing their lives, according to Jesus). But those whose aim is Jesus'

glory, who want to point to Him in all they do, whose aim and greatest joy is to reveal Jesus – to those Jesus entrusts his Spirit and the capacity to live supernatural lives that point to Him! It is all about Him and his kingdom!

So we need not panic about not having the ability to heal people, or raise people from the dead or drive out demons. It is not about our abilities! We don't need to worry about not having any special gifts or abilities. It is not about what we can or can't do. It is about being open to the Holy Spirit and about allowing him to work through us.

Surrendering to Jesus

We are not called just to stand passively by and watch his story unfold. If we want to be actively part of His story, if we want to step into the greater things Jesus is calling us to do as his kingdom's agents, the first thing we need to do is to choose to do so. We need to choose to want to be his Kingdom's agents, we need to say "yes". We need to choose to submit our wills to His.

If we choose to follow Jesus and to step into the greater things he has called us to do, it means saying goodbye to distractions. It is saying to Jesus: "You are the most important person and pursuit in my life and I will go anywhere you take me!" (Jesus may choose to test this! He may want to know if we really mean it and just how deep and real our submission to him is!)

Surrender to Jesus is letting go of what ties us to the things of this world. If we can't let go of the pull and the distractions of this world, then we are not in a position to step into the deeper and greater things he is calling us to. We cannot serve Jesus and the world at the same time.

So the question we need to ask ourselves is: what do we need to surrender to Him in order to step into our higher calling? What worldly thing has a hold on us and is commanding our worship and is therefore stopping us from pursuing Jesus and his kingdom? What is in your hand that you need to let go of? Jesus comments: "Whoever tries to hold on to their life will lose it, and whoever loses their life for my sake will find it." (Matthew 10:39)

Similarly, we perhaps also need to ask ourselves what stops us from surrendering fully to Jesus? Is it lack of confidence? Is it the feeling that your gift is not valuable, that your ability or gift is too ordinary for God to work with?

Stepping into greater things

If we want to be agents of God's Kingdom and step into the greater things God has prepared for us to do, we also need to choose to want to learn how to step into his purpose for us.

We need to allow God to use who we are now and what we have now. What is in your hand? What are you already good at? What do you already have? This

includes material things as well as abilities and skills, as well as spiritual gifts. God can work with what you have and who you are at this moment – if your heart is willing.

As we put to work what we already have, as we use what we already have to point to Jesus and to demonstrate and highlight God's Kingdom, then God entrusts us with more and takes us deeper. Jesus once made this point: "Whoever can be trusted with very little can also be trusted with much, and whoever is dishonest with very little will also be dishonest with much."(Luke 16:10) The key is to be faithful with what you have been given.

And as we faithfully pursue Him and use what we have been given to bring Him glory, we learn to become open to the Holy Spirit. We learn to work in step with his Spirit, knowing that Jesus has called us to do just as he has been doing. We grow in our understanding of the incredible role Jesus is calling us to and we grow and develop in our capacity to step into even greater things through the empowerment of the Holy Spirit.

Encouraging one another to step into greater things

Recognising what we have and what we are good at is a good start when it comes to stepping out into greater things. Yet culturally we are not very good this. We have a tendency to put ourselves down, perhaps for fear of coming across proud or boastful. We lack confidence in seeing ourselves as we are. And yet, minimising what we are good at, not taking an honest look at what we are good at, is not being thankful to

God for the things he has given us. God made us and he is proud of us when we use what we have for his glory!

If we want to step into greater things, we do need to pay attention to what our gifts and abilities and skills are! There is no point down-valuing those. The truth is, all of us have influence in some sphere or other. We are more likely to impact our spheres of influence positively if we have a healthy view of who we are and what we have been given.

Equally we need to pay attention to one another's gifts. We need to help others see what they have, and what their skills and abilities are.

The trouble is that we often compare ourselves with others and tend to think that what others' have is so much more valid than what we have. The trouble also is that we tend to think that our abilities need to be amazing before they can be of use.

The reality however is that to step into greater things, God is calling us to use what we have and do what we are doing – but with a different attitude and with a whole wider perspective! With a perspective of His Kingdom!

We knew a lady once who decided that the only thing she was good at was baking. To her that was nothing special at all – baking a cake was the most ordinary thing. But she read Colossians 3:17 "Whatever you do, whether in word or deed, do it all in the name of the Lord Jesus Christ, giving thanks to God the Father

through him" and decided to offer that ability to God for greater things.
So she often baked cakes for other people, to bless them and to let them know that she was thinking of them and loved them. Her cakes sometimes went to situations where people were discouraged and where there were interpersonal strains. She was astounded when God used that offering of a simple cake, nothing special in itself, and used it to help foster encouragement and hope. Again it is not the gift or the ability in itself which is important. It is the surrender and the offering of it and a heart that longs to step into more of God.

And then, as we learn to use what we have, we are invited to eagerly desire more. (1 Cor 12:31). God wants to give us more. He wants to entrust us with more and so we are invited to *pursue* the greater things Jesus is calling us to. It is in this way we learn and grow in our capacity to work alongside Jesus for His glory and for the sake of his Kingdom!

Imagine what the world would look like if we, as a church, were all doing what we are meant to do? What would the world be like if we as church were all living in step with the Holy Spirit's prompting and equipping? What if between us, church was known for serving, healing, preaching, raising from the dead – doing everything Jesus was doing when he was on earth!

What a blessing we would be to a broken and hurting world as we wait for our rescue and for the day God delivers us from evil for good!

DISCUSSION QUESTIONS

There are a lot of questions below. You may want to focus on one particular one, rather than attempt to answer them all!

1. What would "greater" look like for you?

2. What do you already have? How can you use that for "greater things"?

3. How might your perspective about your gifts, skills, abilities need to change for you to step into "greater things"?

4. How would others know you are someone who has been chosen for a higher calling?

5. What obstacles do you see that could stop you from doing this? Who could help you overcome these obstacles?

6. What do you need to do now?

The Sequel

COMMUNITY CELL GROUP

How do we move on from here?

YOU'RE INVITED

The Sequel:

How do we move on from here?

We have come to the end of the course. We have looked at God's story and we have looked at how our own stories fit into His bigger story. We have considered who Jesus is and his message about the kingdom of God, the realm where God rules. We have seen how God invites ordinary men and women to be those who herald and demonstrate what God is like and what things are like under God's rule. We have noted that God chooses ordinary men and women to have a real and significant part in his story. We have thought about the importance of our own choices in that and how we may need to change the way we look at our own stories in order to step into the fullness of the role and purpose God is inviting us to within his story.

The question now is – where do we go on from here? Having considered God's story and our stories within it, how will our lives change? What is the next chapter in our own lives and in the life of our cell, our church, the united church within our town? Where is God taking us from here?

Isaiah 42:1-9

Isaiah prophesied about Jesus:

"Here is my servant, whom I uphold, my chosen one in whom I delight; I will put my Spirit on him, and he will bring justice to the nations. He will not shout or cry out,

or raise his voice in the streets. A bruised reed he will not break, and a smouldering wick he will not snuff out. In faithfulness he will bring forth justice; he will not falter or be discouraged till he establishes justice on earth. In his teaching the islands will put their hope. This is what God the LORD says — the Creator of the heavens, who stretches them out, who spreads out the earth with all that springs from it, who gives breath to its people, and life to those who walk on it: 'I, the LORD, have called you in righteousness; I will take hold of your hand. I will keep you and will make you to be a covenant for the people and a light for the Gentiles, to open eyes that are blind, to free captives from prison and to release from the dungeon those who sit in darkness. I am the LORD; that is my name! I will not yield my glory to another or my praise to idols. See, the former things have taken place, and new things I declare; before they spring into being I announce them to you.'"

In many ways, this passage sums up what we have been talking about during this course. Jesus, described as the servant of God in this passage, is the pivot of God's story and our own stories, the pivot on which everything hangs. He will return and bring justice to the nations. He will bring justice on earth. God called Jesus to live rightly with him and his purpose was to make him a covenant for people – the agreement that God will be their God and they will be his people, the agreement which seals his purpose of uniting himself with humanity. Jesus was to be a light to the Gentiles, to open the eyes of the blind and to free captives from prison. Why? Because God will not yield to another! The enemy will not have the upper hand in the story!

But there is also a sense in which this passage sums up what *our* calling is. God will also take hold of *our* hand and walk with us as we step into being his bride. We too, as his bride, as those to whom he will unite himself, are invited to be a light for Gentiles. We too are invited to open the eyes of the blind, to free captives from prison and to release those who sit in darkness. Why? Because God will not yield his glory to another! He has declared new things and he will bring them about.

Feeling bruised

Some of us might be feeling rather bruised and battered by life, like a bruised reed or a smouldering wick. We might be feeling tired of life, fed up of our troubles at work, in our finances, in our marriages, with our children....

Jesus comes to us in gentleness. He will not break us or crush us. He will not force us into surrendering to him or being agents of his Kingdom. Jesus will not impose himself on us and force us to bow down to him. He will not force us to step into our role within his story.

And yet he persists in his invitation for us to step deeper into his story. God wants to work through us no matter what our circumstance. No matter how bruised or battered by life we feel. No matter what the shifts are in our own stories. No matter how difficult things are in this world – we live in a fallen world after all! Because at the end of the day it is not about us! It is about Him! And in being about Him, it is about us too. God's purpose is our redemption. God's purpose is to see evil destroyed and we united to him. And so God invites us deeper.

For many of us this is not easy! It is hard to focus on Jesus when things are tough in our own lives. And why should we trust God when we have been through such a lot of difficulties, when it feels like he is a million miles away, when we have asked him for things and he seemingly has not answered?

Stepping into the next chapter

And yet God challenges us: "Trust me! Trust my character. Trust the fact that I am Love. Trust that I cannot be untrue to myself. Trust that I love you. Trust that I want the very best for you – you united with me, in the shadow of my wing, part of my circle of Love."

The reason we can trust God is that we are chosen. He chose us and he wants us to be united to him. He wants all of us to be with him, safe in the circle of his Love – not for his own ego or out of any selfish ambition, but because he is Love and because that is where we are safest and most able to be who we were designed to be!

God chooses us because he wants to! God has irrevocably tied himself to us – that is his covenant, his agreement with humanity. So God does not interview us before he chooses us. God does not assess our merit before he chooses us. God does not consider our performance, our strategies, our skills and abilities before he chooses us! He chooses us because he is Love.

Before he knew us, he called us. (Jeremiah 1:5 / Psalm 139). Before we had any story, he loved us and called us. He chooses us because that is what he *wants* to do! That is what he chooses to do. Because somehow it displays his glory! It shows up what he is like!

But now it is up to us. What will we choose to do?

We can choose to remain as we are. Or we can choose to step into his calling on us.

We already have his Love. He will not change his mind about us, nor will he change his mind about his Love for us. God loves us unconditionally. He will not love us any more or any less depending on what we do.

But if we want to run with him, if we want to go where he goes, if we want to be one with him, if we want our lives to turn into an incredible adventure in which we get to partner with him, then it is up to us to surrender and to say "yes".

And we have all we need to step into the next chapter and into his calling. God is there, calling us to himself and lavishing his Love on us! Jesus has overcome the enemy, he is alive and he is coming back for us! And the Holy Spirit is in us, empowering us! All that is required is our own consent. Our willingness to partner with God, to surrender our wills to His – that is the key.

DISCUSSION QUESTIONS

There are a lot of questions below. You may want to focus on one particular one, rather than attempt to answer them all!

1. Within the bigger framework of God's story, what is currently your story? How do you fit into God's story?

2. How has God been inviting you deeper into Him?

3. Has God been calling you to something specific?

4. What do you think the next chapter is for you?

5. What might be the next chapter for your cell?

6. What needs to happen to make it happen?

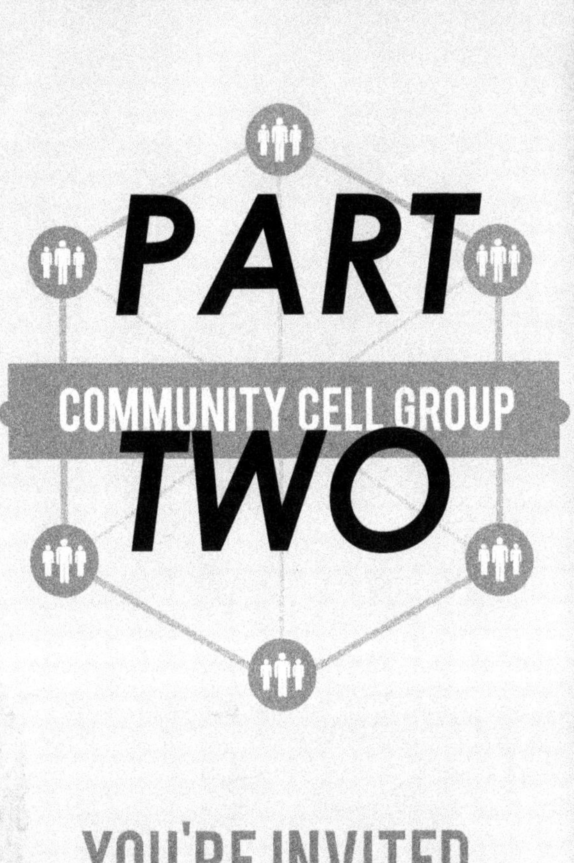
PART
COMMUNITY CELL GROUP
TWO
YOU'RE INVITED

YOU'RE INVITED

Creating an awesome welcome was a deliberate and considered part of this course. We wanted people to feel special and valued from the moment they came in. We wanted to create a space in which people found it increasingly easy to chat to one another and connect with one another. We wanted to demonstrate community and model ways of creating it and practicing it.

So we put a lot of effort into making the physical surroundings pleasant. Cheerful table clothes, candles, flowers, bunting and fairy lights all helped to create a pleasant atmosphere. We used nice crockery (one week we even used someone's vintage crockery collection!)

We changed the church lay out and moved the chairs into a semi circle rather than leave them in rows.

We had special and different food each week, ranging from homemade cakes and biscuits, scones and cream, to sweets and crisps!

We made an effort, especially in the first weeks, to introduce people to other people, to help people connect with people they did not normally connect with.

All this took a lot of effort and time, but judging by people's responses, it was definitely worth every bit. We have learned not to underestimate and undervalue the importance of an awesome welcome. For many people it was this aspect which made the course!

Creating welcome in cells

Creating an awesome welcome in your cells is not an optional extra. It is invaluable. It is priceless and it reflects God's heart.

Because people respond so positively to a warm welcome, it will impact the whole of your group and the way you will operate as a group.

Creating an awesome welcome will require some thought and imagination. It may require some time. It may be something the group works at together.

For each group, the welcome will look different. It is not about following a particular formula which will ensure an awesome welcome. The outward is merely an expression of an inward attitude of welcome. Creating an awesome welcome is about considering your group, where it meets, the constraints you have and working out how, within those parameters, you would make everyone in your group feel valued, and special and loved.

Some groups might create welcome by playing games together, doing quizzes together, doing various team building activities together which will help you get to know each other better in your group. Knowing about each other and getting to know each other more deeply in itself creates welcome. And for people to feel valued and loved, they need to be known and have others take an interest in them.

Eating together creates an atmosphere of welcome. There is something welcoming and special about taking time to sit around a table together and eating together. (This needn't be difficult to organise. Everyone can bring something to share.) Eating together on a regular basis will have a positive effect on the feel of your group.

On a practical front, you may want to consider lighting, seating, temperature, who and how people enter the home in which cell is being held and so on. Perhaps different cell members can take turns bringing their favourite snack / cake / drinks to share.

There are many different ways in which an atmosphere is created in which people feel loved, valued and accepted and which fosters belonging. But not to create a welcome is not an option!

Response

1. What are we already doing in our cell in terms of making people feel welcome, special, loved, and valued?

2. How do we make people feel valued and loved in our cell? How will the people in our cell feel valued and loved?

3. What do we need to do to get to know the people in our cell better?

4. In what ways can we improve the welcome in our cell groups? Physically? In terms of atmosphere?

Thoughts about

WORSHIP

YOU'RE INVITED

Worship is not about singing. Or a particular feeling. Or getting into a particular mental position. Worship is the attitude of our hearts which puts aside our own woes and worries and focusses on Him.

Of course music plays an important part in worship, but every cell, regardless of its musical talent, is able to create the space to worship in spirit and in truth.

During this course we modelled several different ways in which as groups we can worship.

We invited people to lead us in worship. Typically they used an instrument to lead us in expressing our worship in song.

Another week, we sang along to music on a CD. Those who did not want to sing were at liberty to simply listen.

One week we had Bible verses about who God is and what he is like written on pieces of paper. Each person was encouraged to take a piece of paper, and to meditate and think about that verse. People were then encouraged to explain to one another what they wanted to worship God for. Finally people were encouraged to express that to God in prayer.

Another week we used a Psalm as a way of focussing on God, and invited people to express their thanks and praise and worship to God on the back of and as a response to the psalm.

One week we had a more liquid style worship and response time. We set up various stations where people could go, on their own, to respond to God and to connect with God. Some stations were meditative – for

example taking a wooden cross, holding it if you wanted, to meditate on Jesus and to thank him and worship him for who he is. Some stations encouraged self-examination before God – weighing up stones to symbolise the weighing up of decisions, writing about choices and laying them on the altar, using paint to demonstrate our resolve to leave behind good influences and a good legacy.

Again it is not aout a formula. It's about creatively thinking of ways through which we help each other connect with God.

Worship in our cell groups

Worshipping together is not only for Sunday mornings. There is something very powerful about a group of people leaving their baggage behind and focussing on God to worship him for who he is.

Learning to truly worship within a cell setting is challenging but also rewarding. It is the art of working out how to lead our group to connect with God, how to enter into that sacred space in which our hearts touch God's.

The best way to learn is through practice, through trying things out and through talking with other groups about what they do.

On a practical level, a good starting point is to consider the people in your cell. Where are people at when it comes to worship? Do people in your cell understand the difference between worship and prayer? What

kinds of things would frighten them into silence? On what levels could the group be challenged to try new things? What are the small slow steps that will take the group step by step into deeper and more personal expressions of worship?

In what ways could the ideas outlined above be adapted to suit your cell group? What other ideas can you come up with.

It might be appropriate to encourage different people to lead in worship. In this way they feel they are part of things and they are able to lead in a way that they prefer!

The important thing is to make sure in our times of worship, people are able to connect deeply with God, leave their own problems behind, focus on God and worship Him!

Response

1. What does the worship section in your cell group typically look like?

2. What is good about what you already do to connect with God in worship?

3. How can you lead the people in your cell group to genuinely connect with God's heart in a way that suits their personality and preferences?

4. What kinds of things help you to connect with God in worship? What new ideas could you try in your group?

WITNESS

YOU'RE INVITED

All of us are called to be witnesses – agents of God, who explain, proclaim and demonstrate the reality of God's kingdom and the reality of the King, and who testify and tell what God has done for them and is doing in them.

Witness cannot be contrived or forced. Effective witness comes out of genuine relationship, and dovetails with the witnesser's personality.

Lawrence Singlehurst, of Cell UK, maintains that the witness part of cell groups is about encouraging and enabling one another to be effective witnesses to our friends and family rather than to work out (contrived) ways of bringing people into the sphere of our cell.

We have tried to model this to some extent during the Community Cell course.

One vital way in which we can encourage one another to be good witnesses is to pray specifically for one another with regards to people or situations in which we are called to be witnesses.

In order to pray effectively however, it is important that we are open and honest about the situations and relationships we find ourselves in. If the group understands our situation, they will be more able to pray effectively for us to be kingdom agents in that situation.

Taking time to share our situations, to talk about the friends that are on our hearts is time well spent if it leads into the group gathering around to pray.

Prayer for one another with regard to witness can be done in different ways.

It can be done by taking turns – focussing on one member of the cell group at a time, taking time to pray for them and for the way they interact and reach out to their friends or a particular situation.

It will include taking time to listen to what God might be saying about that situation or to that person. It may be appropriate to focus on one member of the cell per week, rather than on everyone in one week.

Praying for one another can be done by taking time each week to pray for each other's friends. Each member identifies a person for whom they specifically want to pray. After a while the group will not need reminding of who each other's specific person is. The group prays together for these identified friends.

It is perhaps important to underline that there is a slight difference between praying for a person according to their needs and praying for a person to be an effective witness. The former focusses on the person. The latter focusses on their outreach and therefore on people within the sphere of influence of the person being prayed for. Both are important within a cell group. But they must not be confused. There needs to be a distinciton made between the two focuses of prayer.

But let us in our groups encourage one another as we learn to be agents of God's kingdom, as we witness to what God is like and as we bless a broken and hurting world.

Response

1. What does the witness section in your cell group typically look like, if it happens at all?

2. To what extent to people understand that they are witnesses?

3. To what extent do group members know about to whom the other group members are witnessing? How much time do you spend sharing these situations with one another?

4. Is there a desire in your group to pray for one another? If not, how can this be fostered or encouraged?

5. What might be the most practical ways in which you can ensure that each member of the group has the time to share? Time to be prayed for?

www.ingramcontent.com/pod-product-compliance
Ingram Content Group UK Ltd.
Pitfield, Milton Keynes, MK11 3LW, UK
UKHW020222250726
13967UKWH00001B/134

9 781291 376463